AF305056

The WEAVER'S TRADE

900 years from Handloom to Hi-Tech

The WEAVER'S TRADE

900 years from Handloom to Hi-Tech

ALEX MARTIN &
EMMA CRICHTON-MILLER

with KIMBERLEY CHANDLER

UNICORN

Published in 2026 by Unicorn,
an imprint of Unicorn Publishing Group
Charleston Studio
Meadow Business Centre
Lewes BN8 5RW
www.unicornpublishing.org

ISBN 978-1-916846-73-9

10 9 8 7 6 5 4 3 2 1

Designed by Matthew Wilson

Printed by Bell & Bain, Glasgow UK

Frontispiece: Samples of ikat weaving by Mary Restieaux. The technique
involves tying bundles of yarn tightly together with a pattern of bands,
before dyeing them, so that where the bundles are tied, the dye does not
reach. The yarns are then woven to create a slightly staggered effect.

Cover imagery courtesy Adamantia Tserkezoglou / Elina Karadzhova

Contents

BUCKINGHAM PALACE

The textile and fashion industries of the United Kingdom represent a remarkable continuity of skill, ingenuity, and enterprise. They are industries shaped not only by technological progress, but by generations of individuals whose knowledge, discipline, and commitment have sustained them through periods of profound change.

Weaving lies at the foundation of this history. It is both a practical craft and an industrial discipline - one that demands precision, understanding, and patience. From domestic workshops to global markets, woven textiles have long reflected the character of the places in which they are made, and the values of those who make them.

This book offers an important insight into that tradition. It recognises weaving not as a static heritage, but as a living practice - one that continues to evolve through innovation, education, and responsible production. In doing so, it highlights the central role that skills, training, and long-term investment play in securing the future of the UK's textile sector.

As Patron of the UK Fashion & Textile Association, I have had the privilege of seeing at first hand the dedication of those working across the industry - from designers and manufacturers to educators and apprentices. Their work demonstrates that quality, sustainability, and commercial success are most enduring when they are built upon a strong foundation of craft. I know because I am still wearing the results of their work, some of it nearly 50 years old!

The weavers featured in this volume embody those principles. Their work reminds us that excellence is rarely immediate, and that the preservation and renewal of skill requires commitment, collaboration, and foresight.

I hope that this book will deepen appreciation for the expertise that underpins woven textiles and encourage continued support for the people and processes that ensure these skills remain an active and valued part of our national life.

Anne

Introduction

A ten-minute walk from the quiet railway station of New Pudsey, between Leeds and Bradford, a small red plaque on a wall announces, 'Spring Valley Mills. There has been textile production on this site since 1794.' Just beyond, a cast iron archway soars above the entry to a cluster of brick buildings. This is the home of A.W. Hainsworth and Sons, a company famed for its specialist fabrics, among them the highest grade of green baize for billiard and snooker tables and the scarlet cloth for the British Army's ceremonial uniforms. The Hainsworth name goes back to 1783, when Abimelech 'Old Bim' Hainsworth first set up a textile business in nearby Farsley. For more than two centuries his descendants have ridden the giddy rises and falls of the British textile industry, contending with fire and flood, boom and bust, technological innovation and industrial unrest, local rivalry and global

The famous scarlet cloth that Hainsworth has manufactured for military uniforms since the Napoleonic Wars (1803–15). It was worn by 'the thin red line' of soldiers at the Battle of Waterloo in 1815. In 1899 Hainsworth pioneered the less conspicuous Khaki Serge that was used in British army combat uniforms from 1903 to 1966. The scarlet is retained for ceremonial occasions: the King's Guards still wear it, as do royalty when in full military dress uniform.

The main entrance to Spring Valley Mills yard, headquarters of A.W. Hainsworth and Sons, in Stanningley, Pudsey, West Yorkshire.

competition. As recently as 1960 Hainsworth was one of fifty mills in the Pudsey district. Today it stands alone. Indeed, Hainsworth is one of the rare surviving 'vertical' mills in the United Kingdom, where every function from sorting raw wool to packing finished cloth is performed on site.

Although the world of Yorkshire weaving has shrunk dramatically, Hainsworth continues to thrive. As one Hainsworth descendant scrutinises the cloth for piano hammer dampers in one room, a shipment of Hudson Bay blankets is prepared for packing in another, while looms in the weaving sheds clatter out fire-retardant cloth for the emergency services, belting for bakeries and lengths of luxurious woollen fabrics for clothing and interiors.

The story of this single company encapsulates the recent history of the weaving industry in the UK. Despite dramatic contractions in employee numbers and a reduced presence in towns and cities, weaving remains a vibrant sector of the

Weavers at Stanley Mills in Bradford (2023). The family-owned business has been in operation since 1890. It is part of the larger SIL group, which today employs almost 350 people at multiple manufacturing sites across the British Isles, incorporating all aspects of textile manufacture from fibre to finishing.

A weaver working on a treadle loom as a woman brings him more yarn. Woodcut, 8 cm × 6 cm, by J. Amman (1568).

economy. It should be much better known. This book is an attempt to celebrate this important industry and cast light on its many facets: what it produces, the people and skills that keep it going and its place in the global system of supply and demand.

Adam Mansell, chief executive of the UK Fashion and Textile Association (UKFT), launched the 2023 report *The Fashion and Textile Industry's Footprint in the UK*[1] with this arresting statement: 'The fashion and textile industry contributed an astounding £62 billion to the UK's GDP [gross domestic product] in 2021, supporting 1.3 million jobs across the country and generating over £23 billion in tax revenues. This translates to £1 in every £34 of the UK's total Gross Value Added (GVA) contribution, one in every 25 jobs in the UK and £1 in every £30 of HMRC's [His Majesty's Revenue & Customs'] total tax receipts.' While this does not equate with the 25 per cent of UK exports that the wool textile industry accounted for in 1770, or the 50 per cent of British merchandise exports the cotton industry accounted for in 1831, it is, in a much more variegated economy, substantial. Of the many occupations required to sustain the contemporary fashion and textile industry – including teachers, designers, product developers, farmers and manufacturers, as well as wholesalers, retailers, fabric repairers and dry-cleaners – the creating and making sub-sector supported 260,000 jobs in the country in 2021, £15 billion in gross value added contributions to GDP and £4.1 billion in tax revenue.

Weaving has been critical to the economy of the British Isles since the early Medieval period. Before that, weaving in Britain had been a largely domestic craft undertaken predominantly by women using a warp-weighted vertical loom or, possibly, a two-beam loom. Raw flax and wool were spun into yarn before being woven into linen and woollen cloths. Silk thread was brought in from the Far East by traders, already spun. In about 1000 AD, however, the horizontal treadle loom began to be introduced into Europe from the East, allowing cloth to be produced faster, with less effort and more profitably. Increasing numbers of men came into the trade, with women continuing to spin. By 1130, when a guild of weavers was first officially documented, a flourishing trade was in existence.

The manufacture of woollen cloth was the backbone of the English economy for six hundred years, from 1200 to 1800. For the first half of this period, almost all this cloth was for the domestic market, with raw wool England's most lucrative export. During

This tapestry, now in the Victoria and Albert (V&A) Museum, London, was woven in about 1595 in Barcheston, Warwickshire, in Britain's first large tapestry workshop. Wealthy families had tapestries, which they moved from house to house, for both warmth and decoration. Most were imported from Flanders or the Netherlands. They were valued above all other forms of visual art. In 1570, William Sheldon set up a tapestry works in his manor house, hiring a head weaver from the Low Countries to train local workers. This tapestry illustrates the story of the Judgment of Paris.

King Edward III's reign (1327–77), however, the wool trade was disrupted by wars and tariffs and this encouraged local cloth production and even an export market. Unfinished broadcloths from the West Country, finished broadcloths from Kent and cheaper kerseys manufactured in Yorkshire were exported to Europe through Antwerp via London, Hull and Newcastle. Trade doubled between 1475 and 1550.

Meanwhile, England's supply of skilled weavers had been boosted by incomers from Flanders and Holland, encouraged first by Edward III, and then, in the sixteenth century, by war between Catholic Spain and Protestant Holland, which saw the migration of Flemish and Walloon religious refugees to England. Among these were textile workers who settled in Kent and East Anglia, where they introduced the weaving of worsteds, lighter than broadcloths. They were followed after 1685 by a further wave of refugees, driven out of France by the revocation of the Edict of Nantes. The Edict, promulgated by the French King Henri IV in 1598, had protected the civil rights and freedom of conscience of the Huguenot religious minority in France. Now Huguenots were subject to legal persecution. An estimated 120,000 fled, some 50,000 of them to Protestant England, bringing their business acumen and their skills in the decorative arts, silversmithing and silk weaving to London and beyond.

An eighteenth-century silk-weaver's loom, with treadles and lifting mechanisms that allow groups of warp threads to be lifted at separate times, permitting complex designs to be woven. Book illustration (c. 1770) by Jacques Renaud Bénard (1731–1794). Engraving, 31.9 × 41.4 cm, after a painting by Louis-Jacques Goussier (1722–1799).

A belt-driven version of Crompton's mule inside an iron-framed spinning shed, with workers setting machines and clearing cotton waste. Engraving (10.6 × 16 cm) by J.W. Lowry, 1834, after T. Allom.

By 1700, wool textiles alone accounted for a quarter of English manufacturing output. This made it the largest manufacturing sector of the English economy, ahead of metals and mining. It is harder to verify the numbers of people employed in wool textiles in mid-eighteenth-century England; historians' estimates vary between 800,000 and 1,500,000 – between one-eighth and a quarter of the population.[2]

Towards the end of the eighteenth century, the urge to mechanise textile production became a major driving force of the Industrial Revolution. A stream of ingenious new machines automated the spinning of yarn and supplied steam power to looms, turning a cottage-based handcraft into a technologically advanced industrial process. The abundance of coal in central and northern regions of England and the building of canal systems and railways to enable products to reach their markets were part of a complex ecosystem that grew to support the industry, especially in the northwest, with a concentration on wool in the West Riding of Yorkshire and cotton in Lancashire.

Equally important for the trade's success was the commitment to excellence in design as an integral part of the industry. In 1836 a British Parliamentary Select Committee on Arts and Manufactures recommended 'three initiatives to improve British design practice: 1) the establishment of design schools; 2) the opening of museums for public edification; and 3) the creation of a copyright system for decorative designs'. The first recommendation inspired the founding of art and design schools up and down the country, while the second encouraged local displays of applied arts, culminating in the Great Exhibition of 1851. The third recommendation resulted in 1839 in the establishment of a Design Registry at the Public Record Office, with accompanying Acts of Parliament providing copyright for between nine months and three years, depending upon the class of goods. This protection for intellectual property encouraged firms to invest.[3]

In 1874 the Clothworkers' Company helped to establish the Yorkshire College of Science, the

Above: Blue plaque on the outside of the Waterhouse buildings, now part of the University of Leeds.

Below: A nineteenth-century loom still in use at the working wool museum of Coldharbour Mill, Uffculme, Devon. The mill, owned by Fox Brothers, began production in 1797.

original core of what is today the University of Leeds. The college was set up to train young men in all aspects of the textile industry – from dye chemist, to works manager to fabric designer – and to ensure that British textile manufacturing did not lose out to European competition. Meanwhile, in neighbouring Bradford, nicknamed 'Worstedopolis', the Technical College was opened in 1882, with a tighter focus on technical textile education. In 1900, a journalist on the *Bradford Observer* remarked, 'If we look around at our mills, our warehouses and our public buildings it needs no great effort to imagine that Bradford is built of wool.'[4]

Within fifty years the picture had changed entirely. The geo-political upheavals of the twentieth century – world wars, global economic depression, the collapse of British imperial rule – together with changes in tastes and fashions, devastated British production. There were approximately 2,000 textile mills in Bradford in 1925; by 1967 there were 825. In 1988 there were just over 200 mills and 30,000 mill workers in the whole of the UK.

The 1990s brought further challenges. Principal among them was competition from the growing economies of China, Bangladesh and India. In 1995 China registered the highest exports of textiles and clothing in the world, its market share 22 per cent and rising. Bangladesh saw its garment industry grow from $1.8 million in 1980 to $47 billion in 2023. In addition, UK textile factories were competing with production facilities in Italy, Germany, Portugal and Turkey that were better supported by their governments, and with businesses in Eastern Europe with far lower overheads. Over this period, skills were lost and mills were closed. Even Harris Tweed nearly went out of business.

And yet, even as the industrial landscape was transformed, weaving never stopped. A deep resilience – grounded in history, family heritage, entrepreneurial energy, institutional support and a long tradition of excellent textile education – has enabled weaving to survive in Britain and flourish in all manner of different ways.

One strategy has been for family firms to consolidate. Since 1958 A.W. Hainsworth has gradually acquired smaller specialist businesses – making soldiers' uniforms, worsted cloths for Hajj pilgrims or baize filled with synthetic resin for polishing stainless steel. Abraham Moon, founded in 1837, adopted a similar strategy in the 2000s, buying smaller firms with new capabilities, skilled workers and specialist machinery.

Another strategy has been to focus on heritage and the power of storytelling to build a strong export market. While in 1969 Abraham Moon was one of the smallest of seven mills in the town of Guiseley, today it is the largest vertical mill in England, rivalled only by Johnstons of Elgin. And just as Johnstons has enlivened its traditional dependence upon tweeds and cashmere through collaborations with leading designers, so Moon is constantly updating its palette of yarns and array of weave patterns with an in-house design team. More recently, Sudbury Silk Mills, established in 1900 but with roots reaching back to 1720, has partnered with design business Dash & Miller, drawing in new design expertise and an international client list.

Rather than competing with foreign producers on volume and price, British weavers and textile manufacturers have chosen to focus on high-quality, specialist products and a globally admired flair for style. Harris Tweed, for instance, was rescued in 2003 when Nike came knocking at their door, followed by Madonna and fashion brands such as Dries Van Noten, Celine, and Maison Margiela.

The survival of the cluster of silk mills in Sudbury – Gainsborough Silk Weaving Company, Humphries Weaving, and Sudbury Silk Mills – testifies to their long-surviving reputation for the highest quality in luxury and bespoke fabrics. Meanwhile John Boyd Textiles, based in Castle Cary, have focused more closely on their specialism, dating back to 1837: they are one of the last companies in the world still weaving horsehair cloth. This has a surprisingly wide range of uses from upholstery, wallcoverings and screens to lampshades and audio speakers.

In September 2022 Johnstons of Elgin launched a new range of home interiors fabrics created in collaboration with renowned designer Ben Pentreath. Pentreath drew on the company's archives for inspiration and was drawn to a palette of colours used during the 1930s and 1940s.

A design project (2022)
at Humphries Weaving
of Sudbury, Suffolk, who
specialise in the creation
and bespoke recreation
of fine silk fabrics.

Horsehair upholstery
fabric provided by
John Boyd used in an
interior by Ezralow
Design (2016).

British businesses have also been at the forefront of innovation in terms of technical fabrics and weaving technologies, whether for transport, space exploration, firefighting, military or survival equipment.[5] British designers and manufacturers have also led efforts to confront issues of sustainability, alongside organisations such as the Swiss-based research and certification organisation OEKO-TEX. The fashion industry has a bad conscience about this, especially at the fast, cheap end of the market: the world produces ninety-two million tons of textile waste every year, and has higher carbon emissions (8 per cent of the global total) than the aviation industry. As fashion and interiors brands increasingly seek to build their sustainability credentials, it is becoming clear that forward thinking on this issue will be critical for the future.

The flowering of myriad niche businesses, selling their designs to manufacturers across the globe, or producing finished products in small batch runs in specialised heritage and contemporary mills, depends upon the strength of the UK's technical and design education, dating back to the Victorian era. Since then, as educational philosophies and the needs of industry have shifted, so the range of courses available has grown and evolved. The gender balance too has almost entirely reversed from the moment in the mid-1930s when Marianne Straub, newly arrived from Switzerland, became just the third woman to study weaving at Bradford Technical College. Leading figures in the UK textile industry, such as Alan Williams of Camira, Juliet

Bailey of Dash & Miller and Harriet Wallace-Jones of Wallace Sewell, credit the success of British weavers today to the education they have received.

Angela Swan, a weaver who began her career at Worthing School of Art in the 1960s, has played a leading role in supporting textile education. She says, 'British art schools have always turned out really good designers who can go straight into industry.'[6] But Swan also notes that textile design departments are much better equipped than they were in her day, owing largely to the generosity of the livery companies. Swan was one of the early women invited to join the Worshipful Company of Weavers and was able to bring a professional perspective to the Company's support for the textile industry. She was a keen proponent of members visiting art colleges and universities to learn of their needs, whether for equipment or scholarships. She also encouraged educational institutions to put forward students for undergraduate scholarships (amounting annually to £45,000) and post-graduate entry to work schemes.

Perhaps Swan's greatest legacy is the 'Making it in Textiles' conference held annually in Bradford. Aware that many students in their final year at university have little idea of what a career in textiles is like, where their skills can be used or what the industry is looking for, she, together with Peter Ackroyd, then chief operating officer of the Campaign for Wool, were prime movers behind the first

'New Designers' (2023), an annual exhibition in London where new graduates have an opportunity to show their work to buyers, employers and the press.

of these events in 2014. A collaboration between the Campaign for Wool, the Clothworkers' Company, the Drapers' Company, the Weavers' Company, and the Woolmen's Company, the conference forges links between educational institutions and the textile industry through lectures, question and answer sessions, mill visits and social gatherings where students and professionals meet.

Over the last decade other organisations have also stepped up their support of the sector. The United Kingdom Fashion and Textile Association (UKFT) was founded in 2009 through the merger of two British trade associations – the British Clothing Industry Association (BCIA) and UK Fashion Exports (UKFE). Adam Mansell, its chief executive since 2016, has become an energetic champion of UK manufacturing, skills and training, an enabler of international business, an advocate for innovation, research and development, a lobbyist with government and a promoter of sustainability throughout the supply chain. Other supportive bodies include Innovate UK, the Future Fashion Factory, and 'New Designers', an annual exhibition of final-year students' work in textiles that has opened the doors to many a successful career.

Uncertainties lie ahead. In 2023, invited to contribute to a parliamentary consultation on the challenges facing the industry, the author and consultant Kate Hills wrote, '90% of UK fashion and textile manufacturers employ less than 10 people. Our industry is made up of thousands of micro businesses who feel unheard and unsupported.'[7] She noted the fragmented nature of the industry and the uphill task of remaining competitive against European counterparts. Chief among the challenges she described, however, were a shortage of certain skills and difficulties in making the industry attractive for young people. This is a primary issue for everyone we interviewed, be it university lecturers trying to move closer to industry's needs, manufacturers anxious about an ageing workforce or students trying to plot a course through tertiary education and beyond.

Apprenticeship schemes are one solution. More technical courses at university level are another. A third is to communicate the sheer breadth of skills required by the industry – from management and marketing to mechanical engineering, from robotics to chemistry and dyeing, from resource planning to data analysis – as well as the fundamental skills of designing and weaving. As Joe McCann, head of marketing at Abraham Moon, puts it, 'All sorts of new roles are appearing because the business is changing. The world we're selling into is changing.'

At A.W. Hainsworth Nigel Birch, technical production manager, is at pains to point out that the mills are no longer punitively noisy and dirty environments. He mentions a new engineering laboratory they are installing to enable them to make their own parts, and a pristine dye lab. He confesses, however, that, for some, the old-fashioned nomenclature can be a hindrance. How many young people would sign up to become a 'top picker' or a 'slubber doffer'?

Even as the textile industry finds its way out of the past and into the future, a remarkable resurgence of interest is taking place in other forms of weaving. Hand-weaving is a hugely popular craft, taken up both by hobbyists and small batch makers. Tapestry has reasserted its presence in the art and design world. Artist-weavers who use weaving as their medium are increasingly commissioned at the highest level and exhibited alongside fine artists. In parallel, as the public becomes more conscious of the waste involved in fast fashion, so they become more attuned to the qualities of finely woven products. Tweeds and tartans are an ever-evolving presence on the catwalk and in fashionable interiors. The last twenty years have also seen new attention paid to materials and processes by a more exacting and conscientious consumer. It is to be hoped that this concern for quality and an interest in how things are sourced and made will combine to encourage young people with an array of talents to consider textiles as a career, and to draw global consumers to British weavers. It is this complex, vital, burgeoning world that our book sets out to capture.

* * *

THE WEAVER'S TRADE

Note

This book was commissioned to mark the 900th anniversary in 2030 of the Worshipful Company of Weavers, the first of the London livery companies to be legally documented. The book is not, however, about the Company, although the final chapter provides an outline of its history and activities. Instead, the focus is on the weaving and textile industry – an industry that for centuries was at the heart of England's economy and still (to many people's surprise) has a major role to play in Britain today, with more than 4,200 textile manufacturers, 64,000 employees and exports worth £3 billion per year.

Given the size of the topic, it was decided not to attempt a comprehensive survey. Rather we have chosen to present a series of portraits – of companies, individuals and university design departments, all distinguished by their enthusiasm, commitment to quality, environmental awareness, high design values, respect for tradition and innovation and, most significantly, a belief in the education of generations to come.

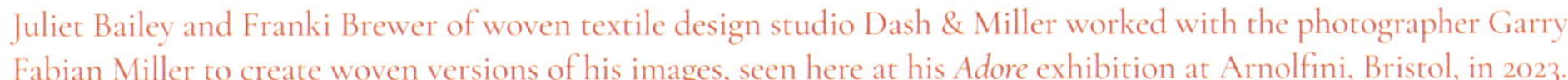

Juliet Bailey and Franki Brewer of woven textile design studio Dash & Miller worked with the photographer Garry Fabian Miller to create woven versions of his images, seen here at his *Adore* exhibition at Arnolfini, Bristol, in 2023.

CHAPTER 1

Weavers of Silk and Cashmere

In 1851 a weaver in the north of Scotland, James Johnston of Elgin, began making cloth from a rare exotic fibre: a light, soft wool that grows as a winter undercoat on the domestic goat of Central and East Asia. Its fine fibres are combed out from the coarse 'guard hairs' of the permanent fleece, then spun and dyed, knitted or woven to make warm and virtually weightless winter clothing. The name given to this valuable fibre was 'cashmere' – an anglicised spelling of Kashmir, the mountainous province between India and Pakistan where shawls known as pashmina have been woven for centuries.

The *pashmina* arrived in Europe in the late 1790s, either with employees of the British East India Company or via Napoleon's army in Egypt, quite possibly both. The shawls caused a sensation in Paris. Attempts to breed Asian goats in France proved unsuccessful, but the wool was imported and spun in commercial quantities in Normandy in the 1820s. Within a decade, Scottish, Australian and American dealers were offering cashmere yarn for sale. Its growing popularity coincided with that of fine Australian merino wool, which was beginning to supplant the rougher native wools of the British Isles.

Johnstons' original fabric was a 'fine cashmere and Sydney wool blend', first sold in 1852. Within a year, cashmere plaids were in London shops. The man behind their production was James Johnston, son of the company's founder, who was fascinated by rare fibres and experimented with the wool of camels, alpacas, llamas and vicuñas, as well as cashmere and mohair. Pioneers in global trade, Johnstons took part in the Great Exhibition in London of 1851, the Paris Exposition Universelle of 1855 and a host of other commercial fairs.

Johnstons still occupies its original site in Elgin: an elegant range of nineteenth-century buildings, laid out among lawns along the banks of the River Lossie. The company was founded here by Alexander Johnston in 1797, originally trading in

Original nineteenth-century buildings still used today as Johnstons of Elgin headquarters. The mill, café and shop are all on the same campus.

oats, linen, tobacco and wool. By 1811 the factory was carding, spinning, weaving, dyeing and dressing different woollen products, mostly of the humbler varieties known as 'duffles' and 'kersies'. In the 1820s Johnstons began weaving tweed, a finer cloth that was either 'blended' (threads of different colours twisted together) or 'district checks' (woven from single-coloured threads). The district checks evolved into 'estate tweeds' for landowners – an expanding market in the 1840s and 1850s, inspired by Queen Victoria's passion for Scotland.

Between 1850 and 1880 the company's exports grew rapidly: primarily to France, but also to Germany, Belgium, Italy, South America and Japan. After a successful few years of trading in the USA, Johnstons and other Scottish mills found their access to American markets blocked by hefty tariffs, often doubling the price of the cloth. Only luxury goods, which were less price-sensitive, continued to sell. Johnstons survived this and numerous other setbacks: fires, floods and failed business ventures abroad. Even the railway, that lifeline of Victorian development,

From Johnstons 2025 fabric collection: daybed upholstered in Wool Tweed Hairline Grouse. Cushions (left to right): Wool Tweed Glen Check in Malt, Houndstooth in Barley, Herringbone in Sandstone, Glen Check in Dunlin, Bolster in Wool Tweed Gunclub Moorland, Herringbone Gorse with Leather Piping.

In 1835 James Johnston (1815–1897) joined the business founded by his father Alexander. He introduced Australian merino wool in 1847 and cashmere in 1851.

was slow to arrive. The network spread far and wide in the 1840s, but the line from Elgin to Inverness and Aberdeen – a gateway to the rest of Britain – lacked investors. It was not opened until 1858.

Alexander and James Johnston were robust characters who stood up to every challenge. Far from the Victorian stereotype of the heartless mill-owner, they were men of conscience. They built workers' cottages, set up evening classes in art and mechanical drawing, and served on public boards and committees. When James died in 1897 he was described by the *Elgin Courant and Courier* as 'of a kindly and social disposition, generous and warmhearted'.[8] His portrait conveys this character unmistakably.

The Johnston mill, first powered by water, then by steam (1868), was converted to gas in 1908, then to electricity in 1930. The ultimate source, however, remained coal: as fuel for boilers in the nineteenth century, for generating gas in the early twentieth century and for steam turbines in 1930. In more recent years power has come from the National Grid, but intense efforts are being made to find more sustainable sources.

The First World War imposed special difficulties: shortages of wool and labour, a vast increase in bureaucracy and the loss and scarring of a generation of young men. The Johnston family was not spared. James's son Charles (1845–1940) was active in the Territorial Army; he joined the crowd sending the local lads off to war in 1914. His son Charles Ernest was killed on the Western Front in 1918. Two years later, Charles sold the family business to two of his employees, Edward Harrison and Andrew Boyd.

Harrison was a man of many talents, a musician and writer as well as an expert in textile production. Looking back on the First World War, he wrote: 'In 1914, our circumstances were very difficult. Almost on the outbreak of war, the Belgian and French woollen manufacturing districts were wiped out... We were utterly unprepared for war on the scale of 1914... Mills that never had tried a night shift managed somehow to extemporise. Every possible man had volunteered for active service and every factory was short-handed. All limitations went overboard, women worked all night, older men did jobs they had forgotten about since they were apprentices. This was typical of all Scotland, and doubtless it was equally true

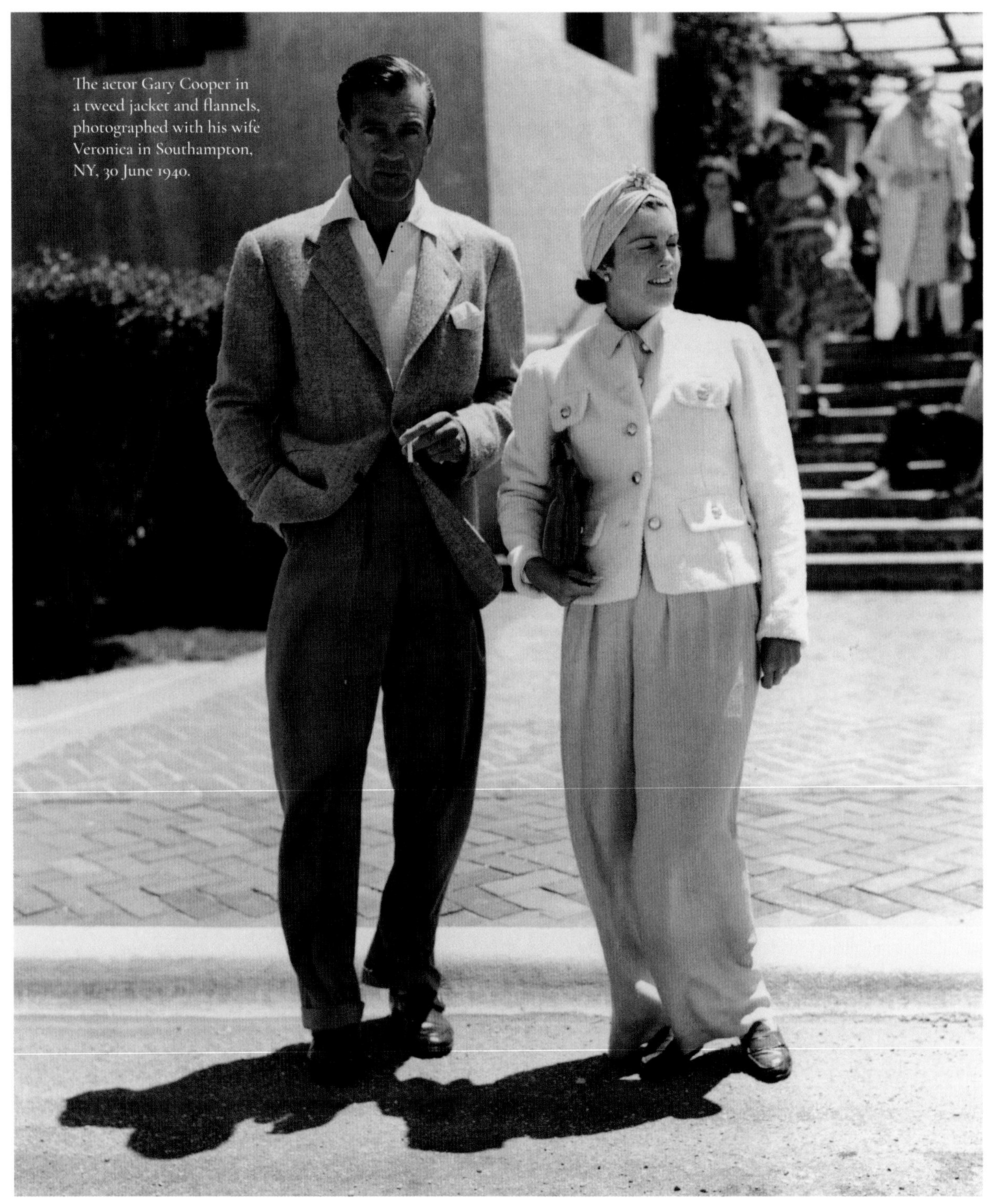

The actor Gary Cooper in a tweed jacket and flannels, photographed with his wife Veronica in Southampton, NY, 30 June 1940.

of England. The people at home were as willing as the men in the trenches – they only needed to be told what to do.'[9]

With the return of peace, business revived. The Scottish wool industry began forming associations to market their products to the world. Johnstons helped to found the Scottish Wool Trade Mark Association (1922) and the National Association of Scottish Woollen Manufacturers (1927). Tweed was suddenly glamorous – for both men and women – thanks to the French designer Coco Chanel, who introduced it to the Paris salons. Famous men – including the Prince of Wales, Errol Flynn and Gary Cooper – took to posing in tweed for publicity shots as they played golf, went fishing or stepped out in fashionable resorts.

The good times did not last long, however. The world financial crisis of 1929–30, mass unemployment, political upheavals in Germany, Italy and Spain, Japan's invasion of Manchuria... Very soon the world was at war again. Shortages of raw materials and labour, poor business returns, fear of German bombing raids, anxiety, exhaustion... all took their toll. As Edward Harrison wrote, 'Glance along row after row of busy looms – where are the bright colours and various designs of other days? Nothing but khaki, khaki, its neutral shade fading into the distance.' The menace of air attack brought a new problem – the black-out: 'an ordinary woollen textile mill has hundreds of windows and acres of glass roof'. Yet Harrison remained optimistic. 'Twice in less than a generation we have seen our sons go forth to war. Again we see the structure of our trade trembling, rebuilt after the devastation of the Great War with so much patience and enterprise. There is no grumbling at these sacrifices... No doubts exist in our mind as to the righteousness of our cause or the final issue of the conflict. The work of two decades falls in ruins, but we will rebuild in a better world.'[10]

The better world was slow to appear, but by the 1960s the firm was in good shape again. Ownership and management of the company stayed in the Harrison family through Edward's son Ned and nephew John. In 1980 they opened a knitwear mill in Hawick, a bold move at a time when the industry was in decline. Its success, which surprised many observers, was ascribed to the high quality of its products and the values of a strong family business. Computer-aided design (CAD) was introduced in 1980, and with it a greater emphasis on contemporary styles. Johnstons recruited the designer Frances Teckkam, whose bold reinventions of tartan, with bright blue, pink and emerald green, appealed to a younger market. A Johnstons' sales office was opened in London, £10 million was invested in machinery, and new marketing efforts were made overseas. Thus, a transition began: from 'a Scottish woollen manufacturer to a global fashion supplier'.[11]

A business consultant's report, *The Scottish Clothing and Textile Industry,* published in the year 2000,[12] provides a picture of the situation at the start of the new millennium. Despite the closure of several major companies, the textile industry was still the fourth largest manufacturing sector in Scotland, providing 11 per cent of all manufacturing jobs. It had a reputation for well-designed, high-quality fabrics for luxury markets. Threats existed from the eastward expansion of the European Union, increasing trade with China and the unpredictable nature of the fashion business, but a strong future was predicted for 'niche and quality players'... Short runs, high value and flexible production looked promising; volume production much less so. These predictions were to prove well-founded.

Ned Harrison died in 2000, his cousin John in 2001 and the chairmanship passed to Ian Urquhart, Ned's son-in-law, who was also managing director of his family's whisky-bottling firm. The Harrison and Urquhart families have remained on the board of directors ever since.

Johnstons' continuing success owes much to its professional managers: especially James Sugden, group managing director from 1987 to 2009, who oversaw an increase in turnover from £5 million to more than £50 million, tripled the workforce and increased the number of designers from one to fourteen. Believing that cashmere needed to appeal to younger buyers, he encouraged the designers to experiment with different colours, using a palette inspired by the Scottish Colourists.

Sugden championed sustainability, training and youth opportunities, not only in Scotland but also in Mongolia and China: he had a particular concern for the culture and welfare of the goatherds who supply cashmere wool. Since his time, the managing directors have been James Dracup, Simon Cotton and Christopher Gaffney. Their achievements are visible in the company's consistently positive balance sheet, outlook and atmosphere.

Johnstons in 2024 dedicated 70 per cent of its production to accessories (scarves, stoles, gloves, socks, hats, throws, cushions and blankets) and 30 per cent to men's and women's apparel. About the same percentages applied to production for luxury brands and for their own label. Elgin is one of the few surviving 'vertical' mills in the UK, which buy raw wool and take it through all the processes of dyeing, spinning, weaving and finishing. They have in the region of 1,200 employees, who perform 380 different roles – an indication of the variety and complexity of the work. The knitwear mill continues to run successfully at Hawick, and the company's retail business includes shops at the two mills, in London, Edinburgh, St Andrews and Kildare. The brand is sold in forty countries worldwide.

In 2024 Johnstons of Elgin received a King's Award for Enterprise and a Warrant of Appointment to The King as Manufacturers of Estate Tweeds, Knitwear and Woven Accessories. They also achieved 'B Corporation' Certification, which demonstrates that the business meets high standards of environmental performance, ethics, accountability, transparency, employee benefits, diversity, equity and inclusion, charitable giving and supply chain practices. The business philosophy, which includes commitments to staff well-being, training and the environment, is summed up by Chris Gaffney, the company's chief executive: 'Our products are made to last and are the antithesis of fast fashion. We design beautiful, wearable pieces that won't languish in your wardrobe or be out of style and in landfill by next season.'

Alex Begg

Alexander Begg (1825–1882) set up as a manufacturer of shawls in Paisley in the early 1860s with a partner, Robert Dalziel. They worked in Causeyside Street, the centre of shawl weaving in the town. It was said that they 'united artistic taste with good manufacturing'.[13] The business prospered and, by 1871, despite relatively humble origins, Alexander Begg was living in a large, detached house in the town's most desirable area. Begg sold the business to his foreman, Alexander Paterson, who moved the factory to the coastal town of Ayr in 1902, where, under the name Alex Begg, they still operate today – about an hour's drive south of Glasgow, and a mile or two from the celebrated golf course at Troon. The company was bought in 1945 by Moorhouse & Brook, who wove cashmere, heavy wool blankets and cloth for men's ties. In 2002 they were taken over by Lindéngruppen, a Swedish family company with worldwide interests in sustainable manufacturing. Under the new owners, Alex Begg placed itself firmly at the luxury end of the market, specialising in cashmere, silk and fine wool, with a wide range of light, luxurious fabrics of contemporary design. A knitwear subsidiary, Scott & Charters of Hawick, was acquired in 2020.

Approximately 85 per cent of production goes to British and French fashion houses and designers; the remainder is for sale through their retail business, Begg x Co, with shops in London's Burlington Arcade, online and at the mill in Ayr.

Ian Laird, chief executive from 2011 to 2024, described the company's manufacturing process as 'a unique balance between traditional techniques and new technology. The weaving loom contributed to the start of the industrial revolution and weaving remains the core of what we do. Technology has certainly moved on and in particular the use of various finishing processes gives the product its special characteristics – and this is much more of an artisanal activity... Today, we employ approximately 150 people, the bulk of whom are involved in the manufacture of around 250,000 items per year. We are continually investing in new state-of-the-art systems and technology, but that doesn't mean we have left traditional techniques behind. We still pummel the cloth in a century-old wooden milling machine to release short fibres for a soft handle.'

Sustainability is a big priority. 'Our environmental concerns are wide-ranging, from the sheep, goats and rabbits that produce our fibres, to what happens to our waste materials.'[14] The company is a member of several international bodies: the Sustainable Fabric Alliance, the Roadmap to Zero programme (minimising chemical pollution), B Corporation certification, and Sedex ('driving improvements in responsible and ethical business practices in global supply chains').

The Alex Begg 'Mini' yacht cardigan for women, knitted in 100 per cent cashmere, available in eleven different colours.

Jonny Mackinnon, new product development manager at Alex Begg, opens up one of the firm's archive volumes of samples.

I was shown around the mill by Jonny MacKinnon, new product development manager. 'This is a brand new role. The design team here are busy full time, so my job is to communicate and fix problems between design and production. I also head up the team for New Product Development through to Bulk Production.' For Jonny, the distinguishing features of Alex Begg are 'quality, trust, commitment, long-standing relationships, and sustainability'.

Design inspiration comes primarily from nature – the colours of fields and trees, the sky, the beach and the salty coastal light. Research leads to notes on texture, graphics and form. A 'colour story' is created. Each new design is named after a place or point of interest in Scotland. 'Things are moving very fast,' says Jonny, 'with new developments and constant change. Before it was "Which of these patterns do you want and what colour?" Now you can have any combination of fibres, finish, weight.'

Jonny is an engaging and unusual character. A prize-winning artist-weaver, he works four days a week at Alex Begg, but keeps his own weaving studio, making work on the frontiers of art and ecology. His piece *Waste Not Want Not*, commissioned after winning a competition held by the Worshipful Company of Weavers, was made from salvaged materials and led directly to the job at Begg. He recently wove a radioactive tartan suit for the performance artist and campaigner Michael Sanders, also known as the Blundering Nuclear Tourist, which featured in the 2023 'Tartan' exhibition at the V&A Dundee.

Other members of staff reveal more of the Alex Begg story: Margaret Parry (Meg), who leads a team of four menders inspecting the cloth that comes off the looms, has been with the company for fifty years. 'I started on 5th March 1973. Before that I worked for two years at the Saxone shoe factory in Kilmarnock. I had no skill with a needle. I was taught on the job by a woman called June Hughes. It was very much different then: we were working on heavy blankets. When we started we made our own pay. For every piece you did, you got a price. So the more pieces you did, the more money you got. I learned to work very fast, because I wanted a lot of money! You started Monday morning with not a penny. You had to work.'

Conditions were harsh. 'See where the shop is? That's where we worked. It was a steel hut. There were mice running about. And there was no canteen, so you had to eat where you worked. We sat on top of the pile of blankets for mending, dropping crumbs from our dinners and the mice running about eating them.'

The work itself has hardly changed. 'A mend out, a short out, a hole... We repair it. But the quality now is much better. Before you'd only do about twenty pieces

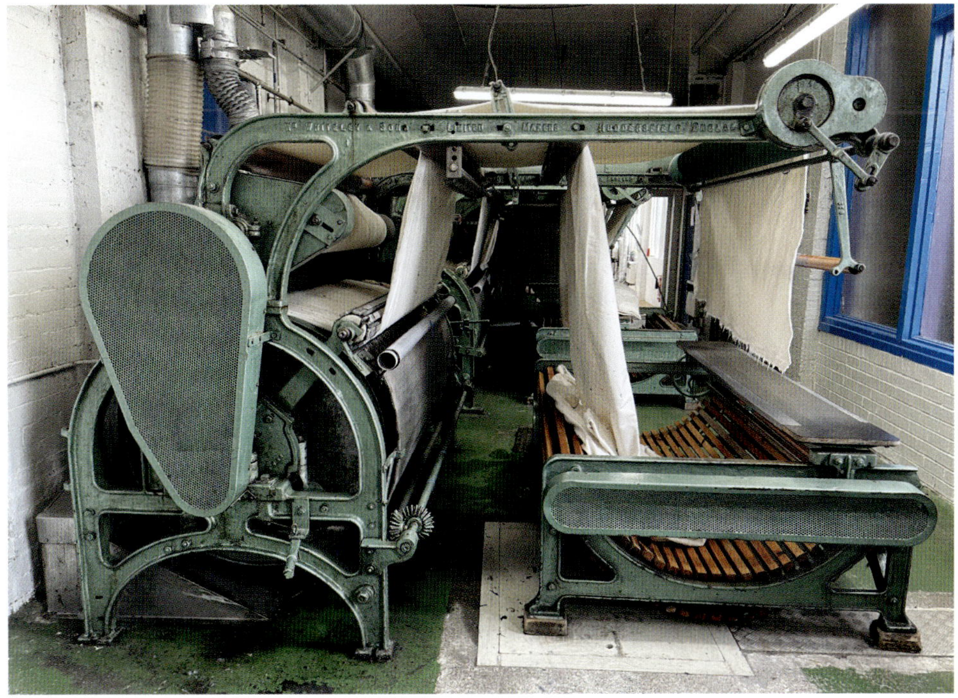

a week, because they were that bad. And they would send work out to menders working in their homes. But now they have magnificent looms, so we do twenty to twenty-five pieces a day. The work is far, far better now. The fabric is checked and checked and checked.'

With the new urge for sustainability, mending has gone beyond checking and repairing new cloth. There is, as Jonny says, 'a massive repair and mend movement. Repair and mend your old blue jeans, your tweed coat. It's very much at the forefront of the textile industry. I remember laughing at my dad's socks. They were different colours. I just thought he wore funky socks, but my gran said no, he gives them to me and I mend them with whatever colours I've got. Now we just chuck them, go to Primark and buy ten for £2.' The philosophy ought to be: 'Buy better and buy less.'[15]

The company now offers a mending service for customers. 'You buy that and you get a hole in it, you send it back. And someone will mend it. Same with the knitwear. Or if you buy something that's getting a bit tatty, bring it back to us and we'll recycle it and give you a discount on a new one.'[16]

Ian has been in textiles all his life. His first job, aged sixteen, was as a carder at the BMK carpet factory in Kilmarnock. He was there ten years – until the factory shut down. 'It was high class; BMK made the carpets for Buckingham Palace, the

Titanic, all that stuff... It's sad. There were four or five textile mills along the Irvine Valley, and they've all gone.' Ian started at Alex Begg as a machine operator in the finishing department. He did this for fifteen years and now leads a team of eight, using traditional processes on milling, scouring and drying machines, some of which are 150 years old. In 2008, he recalls, the company had very few products. Now it has 'hundreds, too many to count. The quality is better too. No one else can achieve the same results because they don't have the old machinery.'

What is special about Alex Begg? Meg: 'We make beautiful scarves! And it's a good company to work for. They treat us very fair.'

Ian remarks on the sense of community. 'It's always been family-orientated. Mums, dads, daughters, wives, girlfriends...We're very close-knit. Family days with a hot dog stand, parties for Halloween and Christmas, theme nights... They're always doing something.' Meg agrees: 'A lot of people met their partners here.'

For Jonny, 'There's a good culture. The change I noticed was, the HR [human resources] department are no longer called HR, they're called People and Culture. They care about the staff being happy, because that will give a better product, rather than dragging people through goals... I was in hospital recently, worried about missing work, missing pay. They told me don't worry about it, you're fine, your job's safe, your pay's safe. Just get better. They ask how they can help.'

As for the future, all three agree that few young recruits have the right mentality. 'They don't want to work. They come in, do their job, go home, get paid, and that's that. There's no pride in the work, no motivation, no passion. It's a shame.' This is a lament I hear all over the country, and not only among weavers. 'There are a few champions, a select few, and you soon know the difference.'

Jonny is clearly stimulated by his time at the mill. 'I'm learning so much from commercial industry weaving, putting it back into my own practice. I see Ian and others in the finishing department, they'll have two pieces of cloth side by side, they look the same to me, but Ian says, "No, that needs raising for another minute, put it back on the stretcher." What I've learned here in a year has really increased the quality of what I'm doing back home.'

It's a sign of the company's culture that a freelance artist weaver can be employed four days a week, an arrangement that not only allows him to develop his own practice but also takes advantage of the insights and energy of a creative individual. The tension between art and commerce will reappear often in the following pages. As this example shows, however, such tension can be remarkably productive.

The silk weavers of Sudbury

Silk, with its shimmer, its flow, its softness and subtle sheen, has been prized as a noble fibre for well over 5,000 years. It dyes well, is comfortable on the skin and has exceptional thermal properties. It has important practical functions in aviation, surgery and war; it is used traditionally for robes that signify power and high office; silk curtains and wall-hangings, and silk upholstery on furniture, create an air of regal luxury and splendour.

According to Chinese legend, silk was discovered by accident, when a silkworm cocoon fell from a mulberry tree into a cup of tea belonging to the Princess Si-ling-chi (a mythical figure; some sources say Empress Leizu). The thread around the larva began to unwind, and went on unwinding for a very long time. (Its length is between 300 and 1,000 metres.) The process of silk production was developed in China and its secrets jealously guarded, although its fame soon spread. It was known

and admired in Ancient Greece and Rome. The Silk Road, bearing its treasures to the West, was established in the first century BC, and inevitably the secret of its manufacture leaked out, first to India and Japan, then to Constantinople, when a pair of Byzantine monks smuggled eggs from the silk moth *Bombyx mori* to the Emperor Justinian in 552 AD. The moths were successfully bred, and the art of making silk spread to Europe.

From small beginnings in the Middle Ages, the weaving of silk in Britain grew into a major trade with the arrival of Huguenot craftsmen from France at the end of the seventeenth century. It rose to a peak in the eighteenth century, when the East London district of Spitalfields was its capital. An estimated 4,000 handlooms were worked by journeymen weavers and their families in that area. They supplied the silk merchants and master weavers whose handsome houses are now regarded as treasures of London's domestic architecture.

The weavers had settled in Spitalfields because it lay outside the jurisdiction of the City of London and its guilds. Their prosperity lasted less than a century. By the 1770s they were under threat – from mechanised production systems, cheap foreign imports and the unintended effects of the Spitalfields Acts, which, over fifty years (1773–1824), fixed minimum wages for workers in the area. Faced with high production costs imposed by law, the master weavers and silk merchants moved out of London; some to the weaving and spinning towns in the north and west, others to East Anglia, which offered rivers for the transport of goods, freedom from legal restrictions and proximity to the capital. Here silk weaving was able to thrive again. It did so for 100 years before dwindling to near extinction in the late twentieth century.

The leading names of East Anglian silk production were Courtauld, Warner and Walters. Courtauld, with mills in Essex, grew from specialists in black funeral crepe to a vast manufacturing empire of textiles, chemicals and synthetic fibres. The family were of Huguenot origin, craftsmen in silver and fine fabrics. Their wealth and passion for the arts led to the establishment of the Courtauld Institute and Gallery in London. The family's connection with weaving ended, however, in 2000.

A master weaver from Warner & Sons working a loom at an
exhibition hosted by the Silk Association of Great Britain and
Ireland, held at the Prince's Skating Club, Knightsbridge, June 1912.
Warner & Sons was Britain's leading weaver of silk at that time.

Warner & Sons, founded in London in 1870, moved to Essex in 1895, supplying silk for palaces, embassies, houses, hotels and passenger ships. They too had an eye for fine art, and commissioned designs from leading architects and artists, including Augustus Pugin, William Morris, Edward Bawden, Graham Sutherland and Howard Hodgkin. In 1950 they employed Marianne Straub and Frank Davies, whose work would later be seen on Trident airliners and the Cunard flagship *QE2*. They also wove the coronation robes for King Edward VII and Queen Elizabeth II.

Despite this long run of success Warner & Sons closed their mill in Braintree in 1971 and the company folded in 1990. Their machinery was bought by its last Jacquard design apprentice, Richard Humphries, whose story is intimately bound up with the third and longest-lived of these silk-weaving firms, Stephen Walters & Sons.

The origins of Stephen Walters can be traced to 1720, when Benjamin Walters, the son of a mariner, completed his apprenticeship and set up as a master weaver in London. His business – importing silk yarns, weaving and selling silk fabrics – survived the Spitalfields Acts, and in 1860 moved to Sudbury, where it remains today, ten generations later, under the direction of Julius Walters. Stephen Walters

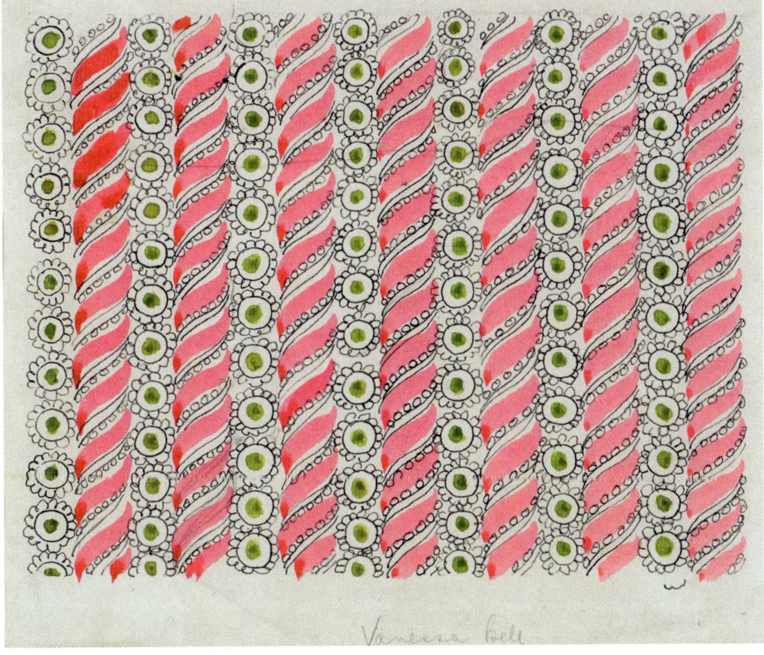

Original hand-painted artwork designed by Vanessa Bell for Helios, a fabric company bought by Warner & Sons in 1949.

wove silk for umbrellas, men's ties and formal wear, retaining an office in London until 1939. Although most silk-weaving companies closed in the Second World War, Stephen Walters survived by developing silk for parachutes, surgical dressings and electrical insulation. They took the opportunity to sponsor five Jewish boys from Austria on the *Kindertransport* scheme. The boys worked at the Sudbury mill throughout the war; one of them, Roger Lynton, later became a director of the company alongside Peter Walters.

After the war important weaving commissions came in: the silk lining of Queen Elizabeth II's coronation robe (1952–3), the investiture gown for the Prince of Wales (1969), Princess Diana's wedding dress (1981) – forty yards of heavyweight ivory silk taffeta, adorned with antique lace and 10,000 hand-embroidered pearls and sequins, with a spare dress for rehearsals and emergencies. In 2011 David Walters wove the cope worn by the Archbishop of Canterbury at the marriage of Prince William and Kate Middleton. The company now employs 100 staff in a diverse range of roles, from technical engineering and colour chemistry to design, sales, HR, IT and finance, as well as weaving. It continues to specialise in bespoke fabrics woven from silk and other fibres: wool, cashmere, cotton and linen. It exports 70 per cent of its production to luxury fashion brands and designers around the world.

Roger Lynton (left) and David Walters with HRH Princess Anne at the Walters silk mill in Sudbury, 1974.

The Walters mill, Sudbury Silk Mills, has been extensively modernised, with forty modern Jacquard looms, yarn dyeing, fabric finishing and a full programme of environmental initiatives under the Oeko-Tex STeP certification scheme. Recognised in 2025 by a King's Award for Enterprise for Sustainable Development, they benefit from cutting-edge IT systems in the design studio and throughout the business. At the same time the mill retains many of its original offices and rooms, with Edwardian glazing and woodwork – a harmonious blend of old and new.

The staff ethos is forward-looking – a common feature of leading textile companies. 'We are all one team,' says Julius Walters, managing director. 'The sales team, for example, understand our design and weaving capabilities, so every structure and every thread combine to create a fabric that delights the customer.'[17] The horizontal layout of the building, with departments in neighbouring spaces, clearly encourages a collaborative approach.

Also weaving at Sudbury Silk Mills, a sister company, David Walters Fabrics, specialises in creating high-quality furnishing fabrics for the world's leading design houses and wholesalers. These fabrics are used in prestigious interiors such as 10 Downing Street, the White House, the British Embassy in Washington, Highgrove, and Kensington Palace. Constantly evolving, David Walters also now produces high-performance textiles for outdoor furniture and luxury yachts. The company was

established in 1975 by Julius's father David, who pioneered much of the technical and design development of both businesses while enhancing their rich heritage in craftsmanship.

Walters have recently acquired one of the country's most creative fabric design studios, Dash & Miller, along with its sister company, the Bristol Weaving Mill, whose work is described in detail in Chapter 5.

Perhaps the most surprising part of the Walters story is its partnership with Richard Humphries. In 1966 Richard became an apprentice Jacquard designer at Warner & Sons in Braintree. Five years later his prospects suddenly withered as the mill closed. An uncle advised him to start his own business and use his £50 redundancy pay to make an offer for some of the Warners machinery. To his surprise, his offer was accepted. At once he began searching for suitable premises. 'I met Peter Walters, Managing Director of Stephen Walters. He must have seen a spark in my eye, because he offered me the use of a house with a 1500 square-foot basement next to his mill and refused all offers of rent.' Richard asked one of the old weavers from Warners, sixty-year-old Bob Mears, for help. Mears agreed to work for free until the company started to earn money.

Peter Walters watched Richard's progress with interest, and invited him one evening to a lecture at the Worshipful Company of Weavers in London. A few months later, he informed Richard that the Weavers had decided to give him an award of £100. Richard passed the money straight on to his faithful helper Bob. Before long the business was flourishing, with commissions to replace worn-out or faded silk textiles on walls and furniture in stately homes, country houses and palaces – both in Britain and overseas.

Over fifty years, Richard has become the country's leading expert on handloom silk weaving, designing and supplying fabrics for an impressive range of historic buildings, among them Audley End House, Brighton Pavilion, Lancaster House, Windsor Castle, Chatsworth, the Palace of Westminster, Dumfries House, the Tower

Gainsborough's House, Sudbury, with walls lined in green figured silk made by Humphries Weaving (2025).

of London and Hampton Court. The work involves thorough research and planning, in collaboration with architects, conservators, curators and interior designers. Accurate colour recreation is a particular challenge, since dyes fade and silk threads rot if they are not protected from sunlight. Finding original colours is a form of detective work that Richard relishes, tracking down historic sample books in estate archives such as those at Hampton Court or Schloss Ehrenburg.

Other customers for his fine figured silks include the Church (vestments, altar cloths and hangings), the British armed forces (regimental colours), the National Gallery in London and the Metropolitan Museum in New York. Humphries

Weaving also undertakes restoration of vehicle interiors (classic cars, the Royal State Carriages, vintage railway coaches and buses), costumes for the stage, community projects, and contemporary design for homes.

Humphries silks are often sumptuous in feel, intricately figured and dazzling in colour, but they can also be quietly plain and understated. The range is set out on the company website, where the story of each fabric is told – from cushions and blinds for a 1924 Hispano Suiza to restored curtains for Queen Victoria's bedroom at Arundel Castle.

Richard Humphries himself retains a young man's enthusiasm for his work. Commenting on a King George II four-poster bed at Chatsworth, magnificently ablaze with crimson and gold hangings, Richard says, 'the King must have needed sunglasses in bed'.

Richard was appointed a Member of the Order of the British Empire (MBE) for his services to the textile industry in 1985 and received the Worshipful Company of Weavers Silver Medal for weaving craft in 1986. The next year he was invited to become a Freeman of the Company, and subsequently a Liveryman. He served for many years on the Company's Textile Committee and in 2016 was elected Upper Bailiff. During his long association with the Weavers he created an Entry to Work Scheme, co-sponsored by The Clothworkers' Company, encouraging textile companies to employ new graduates by subsidising their salaries for their first six months of work.

He has contributed in other ways too, not least by setting up Handloom Holdings, a company to service and repair table looms originally built by the Swiss company ARM. These looms were popular with art colleges, but when the company was dissolved its clients were left with no spare parts, servicing or system updates. Handloom Holdings filled the gap. The ARM looms now have touch-screen programming and are in daily use on textile courses and in studios around the world. In May 2025, Humphries Weaving received the King's Award for Enterprise, recognising its work in sustainable textile production.

Conclusion

Reflecting on the fortunes of the companies that we have looked at in this chapter, it is clear that the luxury market is crucial to their success. The world's great fashion houses demand the best – in quality, service, authenticity, provenance, sustainability and design. Suppliers that can provide consistent excellence in these areas do well, even in a volatile and fiercely competitive environment. The mass market is far less accessible, since production costs in the UK, as in all developed economies, are high. The economic forces were well understood more than thirty-five years ago by James Sugden, managing director of Johnstons of Elgin, and it seems appropriate to give him the last word:

> *'It was clear in 1989 that the bulk market was going to move offshore, and so we were forced as an industry, and as a company, to compete at the top end of the market. We had to abandon making simple things in large volume and make more difficult things in smaller volume... My mission over the last forty-five years has been to draw a line under the decline of the industry and create proper jobs with a future.'*[18]

CHAPTER 2

Weavers of Wool and Cotton

In 1900, the production of textiles was the mainstay of the British economy, accounting for 60 per cent of its exports.[19] As the first industrial nation, blessed with abundant water, iron ore and coal, secure in its territory and powerful at sea, Britain became known as 'the workshop of the world'. Thanks to a series of brilliant inventions, including John Kay's flying shuttle (1733), James Hargreaves's Spinning Jenny (1765), Richard Arkwright's water frame (1769) and James Watt's steam engine (1775), the ancient trades of spinning and weaving were transformed from cottage crafts to fully industrial processes. Work was organised on a vast scale, and the factories – noisy, hot, crowded, dangerous, the air clogged with fluff – were such a hazard to the employees (adults and children) that a series of Factory Acts were passed by Parliament for the protection of workers' health.

Sites in Scotland and the north of England provided ideal locations for textile mills. Towns such as Bradford, Burnley, Hawick, Leeds, Manchester and Paisley grew exponentially as the industry and its markets expanded.

Little is now left of that booming trade. Where there were hundreds of mills across northern Britain, there are now just a few dozen specialist firms. Around them lie the hulks of former competitors – transformed into shopping malls, blocks of flats, hotels, offices or museums. Some, such as the Derwent Valley Mills in Derbyshire, are United Nations Educational, Scientific and Cultural Organization (UNESCO) World Heritage Sites.[20] Others, although not listed by UNESCO, are fascinating to visit, lovingly restored and with working machinery.[21] Groups of local schoolchildren are often to be seen, dressed in Victorian working-class costume, listening to stories of 12-hour days and lives cut short by ill health, or watching spellbound as a row of spinning mules rattles into action. But the history of industrial weaving in Britain does not end there. The scale of production today is smaller, the markets narrower, but textile mills across the country continue to produce high quality, commercially successful fabrics for practical use, despite cheap competition from abroad. How, one might ask, is it done?

Inside a Yorkshire woollen mill, early twentieth century.

John Spencer Textiles

Burnley, in Lancashire, was once a major weaving town. The development of canals, coal mines, iron foundries, water and steam power in the eighteenth century laid the foundations for more than 100 years of prosperity. The town's population swelled from 2,000 in 1790 to 44,000 in 1871, and 106,000 in 1911. By 1920, Burnley had 99,000 looms, weaving (it was said) 'half the world's cotton', while its engineering firms – Bracewell, Graham and Shepherd, Butterworth and Dickinson – were building and exporting 300 looms a week, more than any other town on Earth.[22]

John Spencer Textiles was founded here, among dozens of other mills, in 1871. A century and a half later, it was the sole survivor. Its managing director for thirty years (1993 to 2022) was David Collinge, a descendant of the founder and the sixth generation of his family to run the business. He has a keen interest in the history of the town.

The weaving shed at Queen Street Mill industrial museum, Burnley (2023).

'The way these 19th century mills worked,' he says, 'was on the "room and power" basis. A landlord would build a mill and put an engine in, and then would advertise "room and power", so if you were like my family, not particularly well off but with some experience of weaving, you could buy a handful of looms, connect those looms up to the overhead drive shafts, and rent the room and the power. If you had a successful business, you could attach another couple of looms, and it would get to the point where it was inconvenient to stay in the original mill so you would move to new premises. And so the Spencers went from a mill in the Weavers Triangle [in Burnley] to a new building, then a second one, and by 1920 they had 2,242 looms. It was one of the bigger operations in the town.'

After some 'pretty miserable times' in the 1920s and 1930s, the family fortunes revived with the outbreak of war in 1939, despite difficulty obtaining raw materials. By the end of the Second World War John Spencer had come to specialise in weaving light cotton poplins for shirts and dresses. Their biggest customer was Marks & Spencer, who bought 100,000 metres of the fabric each week. This business continued throughout the 1950s and 1960s, specialising in fine shirtings for M&S, the armed forces and the police. David Collinge's father, Mark, joined the business in 1953, and by 1970 he was managing director.

In 1970 the company needed new machinery. A call for cash went out to the shareholders, and although the business was still profitable it was decided to close it down. The buildings, machinery and stock were sold, and the proceeds were distributed among the shareholders. Mark Collinge wanted to keep the business going, however. 'He borrowed money, put his house on the line, and took on 35 of the 600 employees and 112 of the 650 looms.'

David did not at first want to join the family business. He trained as a photographer and worked for a local newspaper. When his father announced his intention to sell up, since none of the family were interested, David had a change of heart. In 1986 he began studying for a degree in textile technology while working three days a week at the mill.

At that time Liberty of London were interested in buying the business. 'We were making a lot of cloth for them. Especially Tana Lawn: floral prints on lightweight cotton for ladies' blouses. They were buying about 1,000,000 metres of this every year, of which we were doing nearly half. But it was a strange business. The fabric was printed with engraved copper rollers made more than fifty years ago, and very intricately designed. The rollers were narrow, only thirty-six inches wide, and by then everyone in the industry had moved on to making wider cloth on more

modern machines. Liberty's were stuck with this restriction because of these narrow rollers. They wanted us to keep these machines and continue producing this fabric.'

In January 1991, Spencers suffered a huge fire. Offices, warehouses and looms were destroyed. They were left with 60 of 180 looms. Over eighteen months they rebuilt the mill and equipped it with new machinery, making wider cloth. Meanwhile Liberty announced that they had found someone in India to make Tana Lawn. 'We had to completely reinvent ourselves as a business. That pretty much finished my father off, so I took over.'

'We had these brand new machines that could make almost anything and a big wide world out there of people that needed fabrics. And so, in a slightly random way, our strategy became "we'll make anything". And that's really how things have developed. We can't compete on price or volume, but we can compete in terms of service and the ability to make things that other people don't want to make. They might be technical fabrics or incredibly simple fabrics, special widths, designs or quantities…'

Much of their work today goes into 'composites', polyester fabrics encased in resin to make low-friction bearings, filters for air vents and chimneys, multilayered fabrics, loudspeaker cones, Taekwondo suits, horse blankets, mats, rifle cleaning cloths, thermally insulated wadding, flame-retardant material, firefighting suits, and high-visibility work

Fabric inspection and mending
at John Spencer Textiles (2024).

clothes with polyester on one side and cotton on the other – 'and these aren't two fabrics stuck together, we have woven two fabrics one on top of the other and stitched them together in the weaving process'.

They have also made reproductions of historic fabrics such as Captain Scott's gabardine coat, or bodywork for a 1920s racing Bentley in Rexine, an early artificial leather.

In 2006 Spencers bought the home furnishing company Ian Mankin, which had been a client since the 1990s. David Collinge 'thought it might be interesting to have an end route to market. It was at a time when we were questioning the future of weaving in the UK, so it was partly defensive, and partly a search for diversification. We thought retail was the panacea for everything. As a

A visit by the Princess Royal, president of the UK Fashion and Textile Association, to John Spencer Textiles in Burnley, January 2020. Next to the Princess is David Collinge, the firm's managing director from 1993 to 2022.

manufacturer we looked at the price we were selling at, and then the price our customer was selling at, and we thought this was outrageous, a licence to print money. We soon found that it wasn't quite so simple. We needed a marketing department, merchandising, sales... Fourteen people in the office instead of two.'

Despite surprises, 'it has been a really interesting and useful development. It was about ten percent of our turnover when we bought it, and it's now thirty-five percent. We can now see and understand the whole process, from design and creation through to wholesale and retail.'

In 2022 David Collinge sold John Spencer Textiles to one of his co-directors, Simon Blackley. The firm's accountants had recommended liquidation as the most profitable way out, but, says David, there was a community to consider. 'We employ fifty people here. That's fifty families, people we know, not just names on a payroll. They have skills that have been developed not just over their own working lives, but over the lives that have gone before them – the people that trained them, and the skills they passed on. It seems absolute madness for something like that just to close. And desperately sad. You don't see new businesses like this setting up, because they are so capital intensive. What you see here is years of reinvested profits, the result of owners not milking the business but ploughing the money back in again. So the accumulated profits are all tied up in the stock and machinery. Simon Blackley has worked here for more than fifteen years. He provides continuity for staff and customers, and I'm very happy to hand over to him.'

Pennine Weavers

An hour's drive east of Burnley, across the moors that divide Lancashire and Yorkshire, lies the town of Keighley. This is the home of Pennine Weavers. The philosophy here is similar in some important respects to that of John Spencer Textiles – investment in new technology, commitment to staff, a bespoke service to customers. Instead of weaving 'anything for anyone', however, Pennine Weavers concentrates on a single product: fine suiting material, woven on commission for

'Prince of Wales' check suiting, Pennine Weavers, Keighley (2023).

some of the world's best tailoring and fashion companies. The raw material is wool, linen or silk, the yarn delicate and slender, yet the finished product remarkably strong, with a soft, luxurious feel.

Gary Eastwood is managing director and co-owner with John Hodges, who founded the firm with his wife Pauline in 1969. They have developed a twenty-four-hour working system, with fifty staff on two shifts a day, capable of producing 20,000 metres of cloth (enough for 7,000 suits) each week.

There were once fifty-six mills in Keighley, as well as one of the great loom makers, Hattersley. North Beck Mill was set up in 1913 by Smith Brothers, making wool suitings and military uniforms. Fifty years later, as the wearing of suits declined, the mill struggled to make money. When the owner, Tom Smith, died in the mid-1960s, his daughter Pauline and her husband John Hodges took on the business. In 1969 they founded Pennine Weavers, weaving on commission rather than selling wholesale, and preferring quality over price. They were joined by Gary Eastwood in 2003.

'Our business model hasn't really changed since 1969. Our customer is the person who goes and sells the fabric; today that is Ralph Lauren, Prada, Gucci, Armani, Burberry, Savile Row tailors. The real top brands. They receive an order, they purchase the raw material (the yarn), deliver it to us, give us an instruction on how they want it weaving, and our job is to turn that yarn into the fabric they want. We have the ability to manufacture lengths from twelve metres to three thousand. If we do it efficiently and effectively we make some money. If we don't, we don't.

'The machinery has changed, the customers have changed, but the business has stayed the same. So you will not see the name Pennine Weavers out in the market selling fabric, but if you go to Ralph Lauren and Armani they know who Pennine Weavers are. We are the primary, and the best I suppose, weaver of fine worsted suitings, certainly in the UK, possibly in the world. It's very niche, very high-end, and very high value. The average price of a suit made from fabric that we weave will be £2,000 to £2,500 a suit. We're clothing the richest one percent of the world. We often joke that a lot of people get disturbed when bankers get massive bonuses, but we love it, because they go down to Savile Row and buy new suits. We suffer in times of recession. Covid was bad for us – no one was buying suits, there were no weddings, no functions or anything. But there's been a massive bounce back in the last two years...'[23]

'Finishing is the process that converts woven cloth into a usable material. It enhances the look, performance and feel of the fabric. It begins with washing, or scouring and milling the cloth to clean it of any natural waxes, oils and impurities, and in the case of wool fabrics to develop the handle of the cloth. After drying the cloth is cropped to ensure a uniform fibre surface, then pressed to give the cloth sheen and lustre, and also to ensure it is stable for subsequent garment manufacture' (Gary Eastwood, Pennine Weavers). Some mills do their own finishing; others delegate it to long-established specialists like W.T. Johnson of Huddersfield.

Why do customers choose these fabrics? 'A lot of it is brand-driven, but we weave yarns that are so fine and so complex that not many other people in the world want to weave it. That's what sets us above the rest. We weave fine wool but also cashmere, silks, mohair – what we call the noble fibres. The value of a piece of cloth is generally down to the fineness, the slenderness of the yarn. You need long fibres for that – not found in English wool, which is short-fibred and coarse. Ninety percent of the wool we use is merino, from Australia: 16 micron, as opposed to English wool which is 33 or 34 micron. We have woven 11.5 micron, which is exceptionally fine and rare. We can also weave quite complex designs, to a high standard and on time. People pay a premium for that.

'The Chinese don't compete with us because of the complexity of what we do and the short runs. We weave on average about 18,000 metres of cloth a week, with about seventy machine changes a week. We have twenty-four machines so each machine changes three times a week. In China a factory this size would probably do ten changes a week, in Italy about twenty-five changes a week. So they are set up for bigger runs, and obviously the bigger the run the cheaper the price. We put in a job today and a new job tomorrow. High value, short run, niche manufacturing. That requires an extremely high level of skill from the workforce, and a high level of investment from the owners of the business, so we're one of the most highly invested mills in Europe.

'When I started twenty years ago we were supplying Marks & Spencer and Next. It was bulk, bulk, bulk. At the time it was good, because it was easy, but the price just gets eroded and eroded because China wants it, India wants it, Turkey wants it, everybody wants it. What we're doing is 150 metres of something exceptionally difficult.'

Staff training and incentives are also a key factor, with a profit-sharing scheme allowing the team to 'benefit from their hard work and attention to detail, improving productivity and quality'. Eastwood is proud that Pennine Weavers is 'viewed as a progressive company to work for and we have made textiles an attractive career choice for a younger generation'.

Gary Eastwood, managing director and part owner of Pennine Weavers, Keighley, Yorkshire, specialists in fine suiting materials.

His own career has been remarkable. After leaving school at sixteen with no qualifications, he took a job at a finishing mill in Huddersfield. He studied at night school for 'A' levels and a BSc in textile technology. After graduation he was asked to supervise the construction of a finishing mill at Nagpur in India. 'It was a great opportunity for a young man. A greenfield site. We chose the machinery, I flew out, the only white guy in town, which was a very traditional place in the middle of the countryside. There was a concrete pad, fifty degrees in the shade, barefoot workmen. Over twelve months we put the factory together: the European companies installed their machines, and I oversaw that; they had good Indian managers but I was the consultant and had to go to Calcutta once a month to report to the board. I put all the training plans in place, trained the workers, and started establishing all the production and process routes. It was fascinating. It gave me confidence that I could run a factory.'

Back in the UK in the mid-1990s he joined Parkland dyeing and finishing operations, and became the youngest director in their history. He did a master's degree in business administration (MBA) while working there. 'Then John Hodges asked if I would like to work at Pennine Weavers. None of his family were interested in the business and he was looking for succession. We hit it off – and we still do. He's been a fantastic friend and mentor to me, and I've been a partner here since 2003.'

Macnaughton

Another family-owned mill that has recently changed hands is Macnaughton, founded in 1783 and based in Perth. This specialist tartan weaver is the world's largest manufacturer and stockist of traditional kilt fabrics, now also producing home furnishings. Between 2017 and 2022 Macnaughton was run by James Dracup, a Yorkshireman with a long family tradition of weaving. Formerly managing director at MBA Yarns, and before that at Johnstons of Elgin, his task at Macnaughtons was to prepare the company for sale – and to find a suitable buyer. The owners, Blair and Jan Macnaughton, lived in Australia. They wanted the business to continue, modernising as necessary, but retaining its values.

The man they found, Simon Cotton, had also been managing director at Johnstons of Elgin. In Dracup's words, 'to find Simon, who had many years of textile experience, specifically eight to nine years' experience of working for the biggest, most diverse, complicated vertical factory in the country, and some of the most sophisticated distribution and marketing models in the world, was an enormous attraction to us. Simon understands raw materials, understands weaving, marketing, design – the whole textile business.'

Simon Cotton was attracted by the fact that Macnaughton 'is not a fashion-cycle business. It has chosen to stay in categories such as Highland wear, which has a steady demand, manufacturing to stock and selling from stock. Although it has a bit of a season, it tends to sell steadily all year round, year in year out. The product has longevity. You know you can load up a factory on a consistent basis, which avoids the kind of deep fluctuations which are at times catastrophic for mills.'

Useful as it is to have a steady market, how do they compete against cheaper imported products?

'Technically,' says Dracup, 'from a pure manufacturing perspective, everything that mills do in this country could be woven elsewhere, but it is the

Rolls of tartan cloth in the store at Macnaughton's in Perth (2023). It takes between six and ten metres of fabric to make a kilt.

quality, the service, the product ranges, the ability to produce shorter lengths to a very high standard, as well as uniqueness in design, handle and finish, that mean that discerning buyers who want authentic fabric keep supporting us.'[24]

Global brands have also played their part: Chanel, Burberry, Hermès, Louis Vuitton... 'They are perpetuating a supply base in Europe because they don't want to lose this craft, these skills and techniques.'

Textile mills in Britain today have to be outstanding businesses, says Cotton, because 'they've gone through the fire. The ones that are left have found their niches. They're good at what they do, they're consistent, and many have been proven over hundreds of years.'

Even so, outside investors are hard to find. 'Private equity is not interested because you can't scale it quickly and then dump it out. There's generally quite thin profitability but very big balance sheets. We're not ticking the boxes for your typical investors.'

In July 2025 Macnaughton purchased Bute Fabrics, a firm specialising in fine-quality textured fabrics for interiors. The company was set up by the Bute family in 1947 to provide employment for soldiers returning from the Second World War. 'They have an enviable global reputation for innovation,' says Simon Cotton. 'The combination of Macnaughton's mills in Keith and Bute gives us an incredibly wide capability and the ability to provide a hugely varied offer focussed on the interiors market.'

Apart from the Bute mill, Macnaughton has eighty employees working at three locations: design, management and warehousing in Perth; a Mill in Keith, 50 miles east of Inverness, where fabrics are woven; and a kilt-making base in Paisley, near Glasgow. The warehouse holds 800 tartans in stock, both traditional and modern. Macnaughton is one of three Scottish mills that specialise in this cloth.

For centuries tartan has been worn as an emblem – of a clan, a family, a regiment, a place, even of Scotland itself. A recent exhibition at the V&A Dundee explored the variety of ways that tartan has been used – as a symbol of tradition or rebellion, allegiance or defiance, or quite simply for its aesthetic appeal. Fashion houses in Paris, London, Tokyo and New York have been exploiting its disciplined grids and free colour palettes since the 1920s. Tartan has political significance, too. After the Jacobite rebellions of 1715 and 1745, the wearing of tartan was outlawed in Britain, except as part of the uniform of Scottish regiments. When King George IV visited Scotland in 1822, however, he wore tartan – making it respectable again. Queen Victoria took the process further: she loved the Highlands and had the interiors of Balmoral Castle carpeted, draped and upholstered in three different tartans.[25]

New tartans are created every year, and Macnaughton's designers offer guidance in choosing a pattern (or 'sett') to fit a customer's requirements. At least two colours are needed, which blend to make a third where they cross; four to six colours are recommended, certainly no more than eight – otherwise 'it gets too busy.' Colours, widths and thread counts often have symbolic significance too: important dates and numbers can be coded into the fabric, as well as references to favourite colours, flags and emblems. The pattern has to be symmetrical along the length and breadth of the cloth, yet it permits an almost infinite variety of designs.

Wool for tartans was once spun from the fleeces of local sheep but for the last fifty years has come from finer wool grown overseas. As the yarn is spun using the worsted system it gives a much smoother, flatter appearance, which results in a neater pleat in kilts.

Macnaughton has now started collections using all British wool as well as recycled yarns, but their focus remains on the finer wools. 'Consumer tastes have changed,' says Simon Cotton. 'What I had as a kid in terms of scratchy jumpers, nobody would wear any more. There's a good reason for that. We want fabrics that are durable, high performance and comfortable.'

Queen Victoria took on the lease of Balmoral Castle in 1848. She and Prince Albert remodelled the interiors with a tartan theme, and a new Balmoral tartan was designed, possibly by Prince Albert himself. The woollen shawl on the right is in Balmoral tartan. The sash on the left belonged to the Queen and is in Royal Stewart, as are the boots on the right. The dress is in Drummond tartan and dates from 1842. (Display from the *Tartan* exhibition, V&A Dundee, 2024.)

HARRIS TWEED

Weaver Colin Macleod in his workshop. Protected by law, Harris Tweed has to be handwoven by islanders in their homes using pure virgin wool locally dyed and spun. The cloth must also be finished locally. Harris Tweed is prized for its vibrant but subtle colours, rugged looks, warmth, breathability and water-resistance. (See also pp. 192–4.)

Sheep grazing on the Isle of Harris. Although most of the wool from which Harris Tweed is woven comes from the Scottish mainland, some comes from local sheep which are rounded up by the island communities for shearing in early summer.

Above: Rèinigeadal on the Isle of Harris in the Outer Hebrides, where the local economy is founded on traditional weaving. The colours of nature have inspired generations of Scottish weavers and designers.

Left: Harris Tweed on the loom. This hard-wearing, many-hued, hand-woven cloth has been adopted by Vivienne Westwood, Chanel, Comme des Garçons, Yves Saint Laurent, Alexander McQueen and many more of the world's most renowned designers.

His Majesty King Charles visits the Lochcarron mill in Selkirk, 6 July 2023. The company's managing director, Dawn Robson-Bell, shows him a map of Scottish clans.

Lochcarron of Scotland

The tartan specialist Lochcarron is based in the historic town of Selkirk, where Sir Walter Scott was sheriff for thirty-three years. The Selkirk Incorporation of Weavers, a local guild, was founded in 1608 and still meets today. The town had thirty mills in the 1960s and now has just three: Lochcarron (with eighty employees), Ingles Buchan (fifteen) and Andrew Elliot (one).

Lochcarron, whose history goes back to 1892, keeps more than 500 tartans as well as tweeds, scarves, cushions, blankets and throws. These are sold in their own shops and at Highland outfitters in London, Glasgow, Edinburgh and Aberdeen. They also do a brisk trade in the ports of Greenock, Invergordon and Kirkwall, where cruise ships regularly call, their passengers eager to buy whisky and other Scottish souvenirs. Lochcarron weaves tartan for a great variety of customers: Edinburgh Castle, Historic Scotland, the Commonwealth Games, the Royal Edinburgh Military Tattoo and

Keith Russell, one of the Lochcarron sales team, spends much of his life travelling – to trade fairs in the United States and Britain, and retailers around the UK.

charities such as Riding for the Disabled Association, Cancer Research UK, and Steps to Hope. Other fabrics are woven for leading international brands and private clients. They weave 300,000 metres of cloth each year, a third of it in heavyweight cloths using wool from Scottish sheep, the rest from yarns spun in England and overseas.

Keith Russell, one of the sales team, spells out some of the logistics of creating a bespoke tartan: it takes eight to twelve weeks from design to result. All tartans are now recorded with the official Scottish Register of Tartans, established by an act of the Scottish Parliament in 2008. The minimum production run at Lochcarron is twelve metres, but economies of scale are quickly achieved: sixty metres is only two and a half times the price of twelve.

The Lochcarron mill buys yarn in its natural colour and dyes it in-house, processing quantities of up to a hundred kilograms each day. Cloth finishing, which transforms the appearance and texture of the cloth, is done locally.

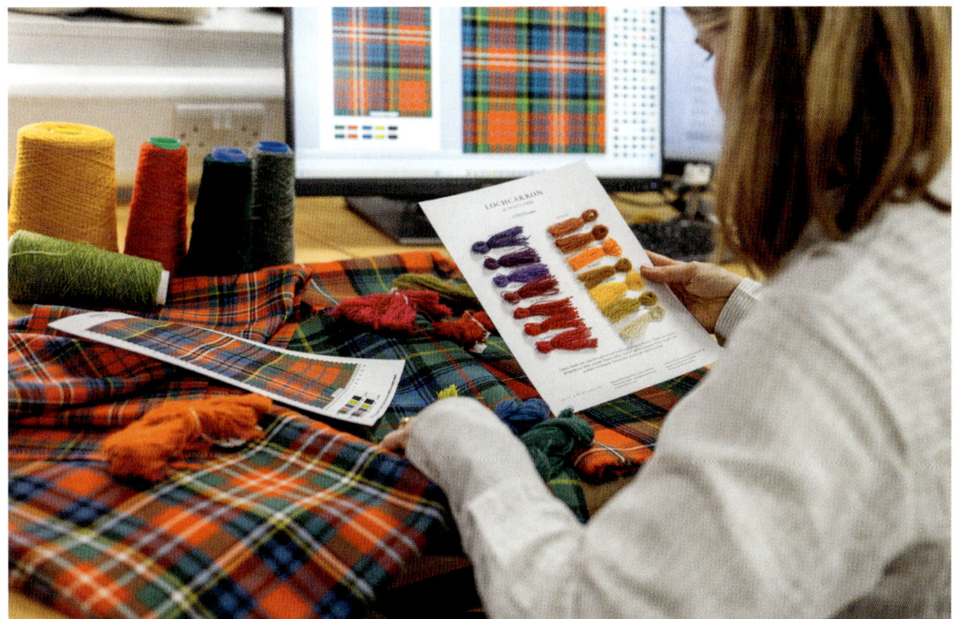

A Lochcarron tartan designer at work (2024).

They sell 'the full highland kit' at a cost of approximately £1,500. There are many variations, depending on the formality of the occasion, but broadly it consists of, for women, an ankle-length tartan skirt, a blouse and vest, with a tartan sash or shawl pinned with a brooch and, for men, a kilt or trews, plaid, jacket, waistcoat, belt, sporran, sgian dubh [a small knife hidden in the top of the socks], knee-length hose and flashes, kilt pin and clan badge.

Lovat Mill

The firm of Lovat Mill, in the Scottish Borders town of Hawick, proudly calls itself 'the Home of Tweed'. The claim is supported by a curious fact. 'Tweed' as a product, a brand, originated in Hawick. It happened by accident. In 1826 a local weaver, William Watson, shipped six bales of 'tweel' (the Scots word for 'twill', a woollen cloth diagonally ribbed for strength) to a London merchant, James Locke, who mis-read the writing on the bill as 'tweed'. Knowing that the famous River Tweed was nearby, he assumed this to be the name of the cloth. Mistake or not, the name stuck – calling to mind the broad river and its landscape, the colours of its woods, moors and hills – and, by association, the ideal clothing for those who wanted to fish, shoot, play golf, go cycling or walking in the country. A cult fabric was born.

Opposite: The full Highland kit, by Lochcarron.

Right: The River Tweed, which for part of its course marks the border between England and Scotland. Its name was given to a local fabric by a London cloth merchant in 1826.

The first textile mills in Hawick were built in the early nineteenth century, when the town was already known for the knitting of hose and the weaving of linen. Water and wool were plentiful, the local workforce was skilled and the town's textile industry prospered, particularly in knitwear and tweeds, supplying Victorian landowners, sportsmen and tourists. Since the 1960s, however, the weavers have all but vanished from the town. The lone survivor is Lovat Mill, founded by Alan Cumming and Stephen Rendle.

Cumming and Rendle are graduates of the Scottish College of Textiles in Galashiels (now Heriot-Watt University). Rendle also has a master's degree in business administration (MBA), which he took in 1985 when he found himself 'hitting a glass ceiling' as director of design at a firm in Northern Ireland. Later, working at the men's apparel company Reid & Taylor, he met Alan Cumming. They were colleagues for seven years. When Reid & Taylor was sold to an overseas buyer and the company's style and direction changed, they decided to use their experience in the industry to set up in business on their own. They were searching for a suitable opportunity when a Victorian mill came up for sale in Hawick – a place, it turned out, with an intriguing story. Built by Blenkhorn, Richardson and Co in 1882 to weave traditional woollen tweeds for the home market, the mill began producing woollen and worsted combinations for lighter-weight tweeds suitable for the hotter climates of the Empire. Blenkhorn, Richardson flourished well into the twentieth century, until the family owners lost interest and sold the business in 1974. It was reborn as Teviotex, making the same products on a smaller scale. In 1995 new owners (a spinning company) took over, struggled for a few years and offered the business for sale in 1999. 'So we came and looked at this place,' says Cumming, 'saw great potential, and by hook or by crook managed to purchase it. It wasn't anything like what you see now, it was a fraction of the size: the machinery was antiquated, and not in a quaint sort of way. There had been redundancies, and no investment or innovation at all.'[26]

It has not been an easy journey. 'If we were not passionate about this,' says Rendle, 'we would have gone the way of the rest of the weavers.' Initially the customer base was small but loyal: people who wanted traditional tweeds, individually numbered. In the early months of their tenure they had a stroke of luck, discovering a set of late nineteenth-century designers' notebooks, complete with weavers' notes, weave patterns and making instructions. 'We stand on the shoulders of some extraordinary Victorian forebears,' says Rendle, 'and we are always mindful of the immense lexicon of weaves and finishes that they had at their disposal. This has been incredibly valuable to our design team and customers alike.' Their reputation

grew. 'We had customers as diverse as ducal estates, British regiments and top fashion designers. From Paris and Milan to the grouse moors of Scotland our richly coloured tweeds once again found their market...'[27]

As a privately owned company they have developed at their own pace, re-investing profits and selling in Britain and abroad, almost without the use of agents. This has proved vital to the

business. 'At Lovat the customer/mill relationship is crucial to understanding each other's vision for the future,' says Cumming. 'Travel and engagement are second nature to the team.'

Their special offering is a combination of traditional craftsmanship and new technology. 'We were able to draw upon our heritage and legacy,' says Cumming, 'and really make tweed appropriate for the whole range of customers throughout the world.' Continued investment, training and modernisation within the mill broadened the types of fabrics they could make; today these encompass woollens and worsteds in weight ranges from 220gms to 1000gms per running metre. While woollen tweeds are the core of the business, they also produce linen and wool combinations, 100 per cent cashmere, and other luxury fabrics. Their stock includes more than 300 tweeds, flannels, fine upholstery fabrics and speciality high-twist travel suiting.

Mindful of the future, they recently invited James Fleming, a former Scottish rugby international, to join the firm. Stephen Rendle met him by chance on a salmon-fishing trip in the Hebrides. Rendle was searching for a successor, and Fleming was looking for a new career beyond the rugby field. 'James asked me what I did for a living, and I told him about weaving at Lovat Mill. He said "That sounds like my dream job." I replied, "No, I must have given you the wrong idea. This is a very difficult business." A month later we met again by chance in Edinburgh. And James told me, "I meant what I said. I'd join you given half a chance." We met a few more times and talked about it seriously. He joined us in 2018 and it's been a total success.'[28] Fleming now leads a team of twenty-eight, overseeing the fifth expansion of the mill. His knowledge of training disciplines for rugby players has proved to be a huge asset. 'We have an excellent development programme that James devised and it's set us up very well for the future.' Every year they take an undergraduate intern from Heriot-Watt University – a token of thanks to Cumming and Rendle's alma mater. 'We live with the constant challenge of practising an ancient craft whilst aspiring to be an industry,' says Fleming. 'Alongside investment in weaving technology we put a great deal of care into recruitment and skills development. Our success depends on maintaining talent for the future.'

Above: A producer of fine wool, mohair and cashmere suitings, Stanley Mills in Bradford supplies branded fabrics to the Gulf States, Europe and the Far East, including China, Japan, Korea and Hong Kong.

Below: The anointing screen used at the Coronation of King Charles III in Westminster Abbey, 6 May 2023.

The design represents the countries of the Commonwealth as a tree, with the King's cypher at the base. The main fabric is wool from Australia and New Zealand, spun, dyed and woven by AW Hainsworth in Leeds. The appliqué wool fabrics were spun by Camira Fabrics (Huddersfield) and R Gledhill (Delph), woven at Camira Fabrics and at John Spencer Textiles (Burnley). The fabrics were finished at Camira Fabrics and W.T. Johnson & Sons (Huddersfield). The linen appliqué fabric was woven at John Spencer Textiles and finished at H&C Whitehead (Brighouse).

The leaves were embroidered by staff and students from the Royal School of Needlework and members of the Worshipful Companies of Broderers, Drapers and Weavers. The screen is supported by an oak pole framework, created by Nick Gutfreund of the Worshipful Company of Carpenters. The screen was designed by Aidan Hart and funded by the City of London Corporation and the City livery companies. The lettering is a combination of classical and modern styles, inspired by Trajan's Column in Rome and the work of Welsh calligrapher David Jones.

CHAPTER 3

Weavers of Technical Textiles

We live and work among hard surfaces – wood, concrete, stone, brick, glass, metal and plastics. Our use of textiles to soften those surfaces, providing warmth, comfort and colour, is there for everyone to see. There is another class of textiles, however, that is little seen or appreciated, and the modern economy depends on them: they are found in cars, trains, lorries, aeroplanes, bridges, factories, hospitals, the food and pharmaceutical industries, protective clothing and equipment for emergency services and armed forces. All have requirements for strong, light, flexible materials. These tend to be made from synthetic not natural fibres – created in laboratories in a series of experiments that began in the early nineteenth century and were first commercially exploited as 'nylon' in 1940s America. Such textiles provide the hidden internal structure of modern life.

What is even more surprising, in post-industrial Britain, is that some of the best manufacturers in this field are British. Little known by the public, they research, design and create reliable high-performance materials and export them around the world, even to India and China. Through partnerships with universities, a range of technical, scientific and design expertise is brought into play. Financial help is given to such partnerships through Innovate UK, a research and innovation agency funded by the government. More encouragement, such as value added tax (VAT)-refund schemes, export support and a 'buy British' rather than 'buy cheapest' protocol for state organisations, would result in further growth of this exceptionally dynamic sector.[29]

In this chapter, we will look at three British companies: Heathcoat Fabrics, Arville Textiles, and Camira.

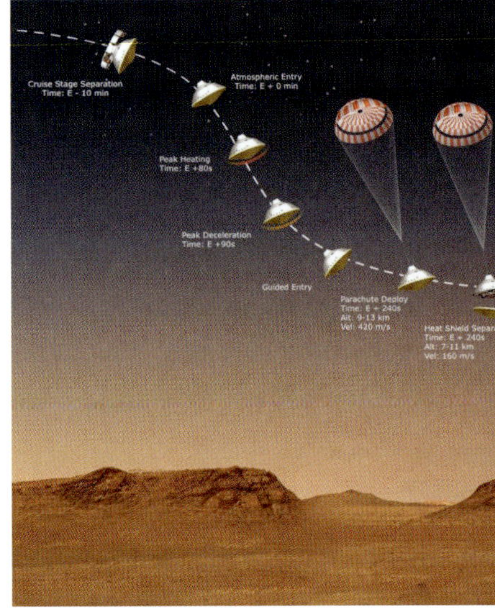

Heathcoat Fabrics

The task was to land a wheeled vehicle, weighing a ton, with its delicate load of cameras, motors, solar panels, transceivers and scientific equipment, on the surface of the planet Mars. Bundled up with a heat shield and a sky-crane, the vehicle, known as the Perseverance Rover, would enter the atmosphere of Mars on the morning of 18 February 2021 at a speed of nearly 20,000 kilometres per hour. Decelerating through friction and compression over the next four minutes to 420 metres per second (1512 km/hr), it needed to slow down further to 30 m/s (108 km/hr) before a powered descent through the last 2,000 metres to touchdown. That deceleration from 420 to 30 m/s was the job of the parachute. It required a fabric that would withstand ferocious strain as it flew open 10 kilometres above the surface of Mars, known affectionately as 'the planet of death' for its capacity to destroy approaching spacecraft.

Anxiously watched by teams on Earth, the landing worked to perfection. The parachute fabric was the work of an English company, Heathcoat Fabrics. No other company was able to achieve this result – a fact that seems all the more extraordinary when one considers that Heathcoat's origins lay in eighteenth-century English lacemaking. The company was founded by John Heathcoat,

The descent of the Perseverance Rover on to the surface of Mars, 18 February 2021. The parachute, made of fabric engineered in England, slowed down the Rover from 1512 to 108 km/hr.

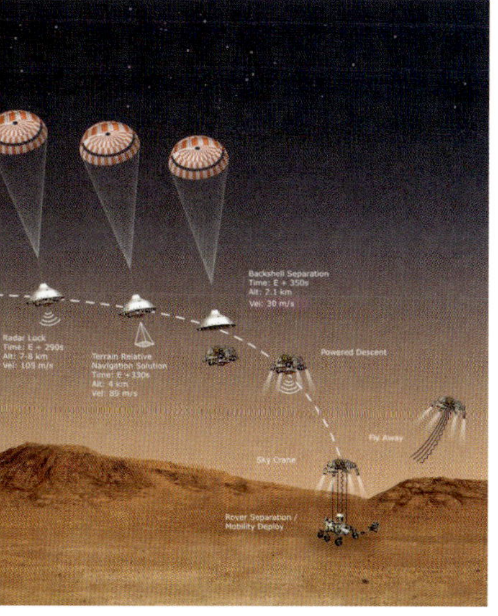

Above: Rapid inflation testing of a space parachute at NASA Ames Facility.

John Heathcoat's
'Lace Manufactory'
in Tiverton, c. 1835.

an inventor and businessman from Leicestershire, who lived from 1783 to 1861. Heathcoat's particular genius was in translating the manual skills of the artisan into the automated actions of a machine. He studied the hand-movements of women making lace and devised a way of reproducing it mechanically. Lace was a popular product, and his factory in Loughborough was a huge commercial success. In 1816 it attracted the attention of the Luddites – opponents of industrialisation – who smashed his machines and burned his stocks of lace.[30] Heathcoat was offered £10,000 compensation on condition that he re-invested locally. Fearing more violence, he refused the money and bought a woollen mill in Tiverton, two hundred miles away, offering his workers jobs if they would join him. At least one hundred families walked from Loughborough to start a new life in Devon.

Here again his business prospered, making lace and crêpe – fashionable materials throughout the Victorian age – until demand collapsed at the end of the First World War. In 1925 Heathcoat Fabrics added weaving to their capabilities and installed their first looms. This saved them from closure. They specialised in parachute material during the Second World War, first using silk, later nylon. More lean years followed the War. Heathcoat Fabrics evolved into a technical textiles specialist in the 1980s.

Heathcoat Fabrics today employs 475 people and has global sales of £70 million. Of these 43 per cent go to Europe, 34 per cent to the UK, 13 per cent to North America and 10 per cent to the rest of the world. Monthly production output in 2024 was 750 kilometres. Capabilities include yarn processing, warping, weaving, warp knitting, fabric dyeing, chemical enhancements and specialist finishing. They have their own research laboratories and a team of development engineers on site.

The range of fabrics produced and their applications is immense. For the automotive industry they weave fabrics for turbo-hoses and connectors, belts for drives, transmission and timing, textiles for bonnets and interiors, seals, diaphragms, spacer material for seats, damper-fabric for speakers, air-sprung suspension systems, and fire-retardant barriers. These are exported to major automobile manufacturers worldwide, notably in Italy, Germany, China, India and the United States. High-profile end customers include Ferrari and Harley-Davidson.

In aviation, lightweight composite materials made of resin and fabric are increasingly replacing metal for both structural and machine parts. Heathcoat makes fabric for composites used in wings, fuselages, rotor blades and engine parts as well as textiles for aircraft seats, ventilation and ducting, and seals for airlocks. A speciality of the company is fabric-to-rubber bonding achieved without the use of harmful solvents. For space exploration they have developed parachute material made of what they modestly call 'the lightest, strongest fabric known to man'.[31] Among their clients are the National Aeronautics and Space Administration (NASA), the European Space Agency, Blue Origin and many smaller private space companies. These innovations have opened the door to other space parachute projects, such as returning cargo and astronauts to Earth from the International Space Station.

Military grade textiles, also used by police and fire services, are a key part of their production. Flame-proof, shock absorbent, waterproof, printed with disruptive (that is, camouflage) patterns, these textiles also protect from the violence of war: fragmentation, slashing, ballistic and CBRN (chemical, biological, radiological and nuclear) attack. Specialist treatments include anti-microbial, anti-odour, chemical-repellent, infrared-reflective, petrol-resistant, rot-proof, anti-ultra-violet and water repellent; among these are their trade-marked 'NeutraliZR' fabrics for CBRN garments, which are PFAS-free.[32] Load-bearing meshes are created for pockets, breathable panels, vests, backpacks, stretchers and hammocks. Meshes are also used in Multi-Spectral Camouflage, which resists detection by radar and infra-red imaging.

Protective military clothing woven by Heathcoat Fabrics in Devon (2025).

The healthcare industry also requires specialist textiles, and the company supplies fabric for patient handling, wound dressings, mattresses and bed linen. Meshes and other fabrics are bought by leading childcare brands for baby carriers, travel cots, baby bouncers and mattresses.

Niche markets include sails for classic boats, fireproof fabric for gangways between train carriages, drive belts for wind turbines, puncture-resistant fabrics for bicycle tyres, chutes for drag racing cars, airbags for motorbike riders, geo-textiles for flood defences and – reflecting the company's origins – tulle for bridal outfitters, ballet companies and theatrical costume designers.

Another notable application was a set of acoustic panels fitted above the stage at the Royal Festival Hall in London in 2007. 'Apparently,' says Peter Hill, 'the timber over-stage reflector designed by the original architects was considered a major problem by musicians and conductors alike as it was so good at pushing sound from the stage to the audience that acoustic musicians and orchestras couldn't hear themselves play. We were tasked with producing a flame-retardant fabric with the required density and air permeability for the adjustable fabric reflectors which throw high frequency sound back to the stage immediately, giving precision, but are permeable to mid and low frequency sound, giving warmth.' The broad range of applications reflects the interests of the company's staff in fields such as music, space exploration, cars, sustainability or defence. 'This makes the work more enjoyable and also rewarding when we see the fabrics we have worked on in action.'[33]

The factory in Tiverton is a highly organised place: spacious, clean, well-lit, the work-flow logical and smooth, the staff calmly concentrating on their tasks. Professionalism, pride and a problem-solving attitude seem to run through the workforce. Innovation and research, and a belief in going beyond the requirements of a job, are integral to the company's spirit.

One of the most intriguing sections of the factory is dedicated to XTEX yarn. This is an aramid (strong, heat-resistant synthetic fibre), bought from US (DuPont) or Japanese (Teijin) suppliers and treated by texturising, twisting, winding or covering to produce controlled stretch yarns for textiles with properties such as elongation at a set load, weight and fabric porosity, according to customer requirements.

In the company offices, I am treated to a presentation on Heathcoat's past and present by John Stimpson. Despite his opaque job title ('Woven Industrial Solutions Business Manager'), his presentation is informative and entertaining.

He runs through the company's varied portfolio, providing two important clues to its success: high standards in research, production and sustainability, and what he calls 'consultative selling': discussions with customers about their requirements, sometimes lasting several years (fifteen in the case of some fabrics for space travel). 'NASA came to see us at a trade fair. Their US-sourced fabric wasn't performing well. They wanted double the strength and no more weight, plus major heat resistance. We exceeded the brief and got the job.' This patiently developed relationship of trust, and a determination to satisfy the customer's needs, explain why they are able to reverse the usual flow of trade. 'We save them a fortune because we give them what they want, and it works.'

Sustainability is a major component of the company philosophy. As Stimpson says, 'We have rogered the planet. Let's give the young the tools to un-roger

THE WEAVER'S TRADE

it.'[34] Three-quarters of the mill's energy needs are generated through on-site solar, hydro-electric and combined heat and power installations; an air purification system minimises atmospheric pollution; there are waste water and effluent treatment plants; and landfill is dwindling to zero. They are developing 'greener chemistry' and increasing the use of recycled and natural yarns. An environmental management team supervises these initiatives, and many of the fabrics conform now to OEKO-TEX Standard 100. The effort is visible in small details, such as the phasing out of fork-lift vehicles: transport of heavy items is on wheeled frames that are pushed by hand.

Top: John Stimpson, woven industrial solutions business manager, describes some specialist applications of Heathcoat fabrics: drive belts for wind turbines, flood barriers in the Venetian Lagoon, healthcare, gas safety, railways, classic yacht sails, parachutes, bicycle tyres, accessories (2025).

Middle: Bobbin frames wheeled around the Heathcoat Fabrics factory by hand – part of a policy to reduce dependence on powered vehicles (2025).

Bottom: January 2023: The Lord Lieutenant of Devon, David Fursdon, presents the managing director of Heathcoat Fabrics, Cameron Harvie, with a Queen's Award for Enterprise in recognition of achievements in textile innovation.

Arville Textiles

Arville was founded in 1954 by William Wight, who ran a business carrying goods between Yorkshire and Scotland in war-surplus lorries. On one of his trips, he met a weaver who convinced him there was money to be made in textiles woven from synthetic fibres. He recruited Eddie Fegan from British Ropes Ltd as managing director, and set up a textile business in Harrogate. They began as commission weavers, making uniforms for public transport staff. They progressed to general textiles for industrial customers, using new man-made fibres as these came on to the market. Their speciality was 'knowing the right fibre for the job': its properties, where to source it and how it would behave in different environments. In the early 1960s they moved to a new site near Wetherby, which is still their headquarters today. Eddie Fegan's son Neil joined the company at age sixteen and made his career there, retiring as technical director in 2024 – 'a man of encyclopaedic knowledge', according to the company's recently retired managing director, Jim Wight.[35]

Despite the purely functional nature of these fabrics, used in Defence, Aerospace, Pharmaceutical, Automotive, Medical and Industrial applications, they have their own aesthetic appeal.

Jim Wight is one of the founder's grandsons. He worked in investment banking in London for twenty years before moving to Arville as managing director in 2012. Since then he has modernised the company's operations, converting from paper to digital administration and, as he puts it, 'getting the knowledge out of people's heads and into the system'. He retired in 2025, handing over to a new chief executive, Steve Gill. Arville now employs 105 staff across four businesses: weaving (Wetherby), coatings (Bury), fabrications (cutting and sewing) in Bradford, and belting (conveyor belts for the baking industry) at Dursley in Gloucestershire. Turnover is approximately £15 million per year, with exports to fifty countries, their strongest markets being the UK and Europe.

Arville's products cover a similar range to Heathcoat's: Defence, Aerospace, Pharmaceutical, Automotive, Medical, Industrial – plus Filtration and Food. Their most high-profile contracts to date are for Martin-Baker ejector seats, used in fighter aircraft around the world, suspension fabrics for Toyota cars and emergency flotation bags for Marine One, the US Presidential helicopter. Behind these headlines, however, there are plenty of quieter achievements.

Jim Wight describes the company's strengths and challenges: 'We're very good technically, we solve problems, we have excellent supply chain security both in Europe and Asia, and our staff stay with us for years. We're a real family business with an incredible technical heritage. Now we need to get better at commercialising and marketing our knowledge.' For this purpose, in September 2024 they took on a new chief commercial officer, Andy Wheatley, whose past life included twenty-five years as a brand strategist, advising many of the world's leading brands.

This was his first experience of the textile industry. 'Of all the industries I've been involved in,' he says, 'this is the most down to earth. A lot of it is to do with the tangible nature of the product. If we have meetings with people, they will be textile specialists and the first thing they'll do is pick up the fabric and feel it, look at the weave. There's an inherent integrity, a "salt of the earth" nature to the industry.'

He is fascinated by the multitude of uses for textiles in today's world: 'The wheels of industry cannot turn without them. There are so many things that consumers take for granted. If these textiles weren't there, they just wouldn't work. I didn't know, for example, that our textiles are sitting in the wings of the European fighter jet. It just wouldn't have crossed my mind that these materials are there, and how tough they are. It's almost going on whilst you sleep: all these critical materials being made by this small band of incredibly inventive companies.'

The quality of the products creates its own challenges for marketing. 'It's an industry that is focused very much on what it *does*. And has huge pride in it. But if you look at the marketing material that goes into it and compare it to the campaigns that go into selling consumer products, it's not as advanced.' He found the approach old-fashioned: 'the sort of thing I haven't done since the 1990s – sending out a little desk jotter so people can think of us when they buy their next seating fabric'. This means there is an opportunity, although not for a 'marketing-heavy' strategy. 'People would see through it. My job is to find a strategy for us that works, and reflects the reality of the business. We make a lot of highly specialised textiles that are mission-critical. You can't just rattle them off. A client will ask us for a specific textile that will do a specific job with a specific piece of, say, military equipment. If these textiles fail, lives are at risk.'

The specialised product, a relationship of trust with the customer, and 'commercially relevant conversations' are his answer to the question that underlies the work of every weaver in this book: how do you survive in a global market?

His ambition for the business is 'for us to be seen as one of the fastest moving, most progressive textile manufacturers... working with others to promote British industry with pride. We've got so much to be proud of. A great tradition. We can claim, quite comfortably, to have some of the most knowledgeable people about technical textiles in the world.'

On sustainability, he has outspoken views: 'There are a number of issues with it. One is what they call "noble cause corruption", which is when people think they are doing a good thing when in fact they aren't. Last year, to give you a hackneyed example, more plastic was produced than at any point in human history, but you wouldn't know that because everyone thinks "I'm recycling my plastics, so it's OK, right?" It's very far from OK. An experiment was made where they put a GPS [global positioning system] into some plastic to see what happens when you throw it away. And it's pretty frightening. Often it ends up in a landfill in Indonesia. So it has achieved a target, but it's farmed out to somebody else. And next year plastic production will go up again.'

So what is the solution? In his view, there needs to be a gradual approach. 'By its very nature industrial production creates pollution. We can't miraculously make an industry 100% green over night. There's a message to go out there: it has to be step by step, rather than these overbearing campaigns.' For a specialist in technical textiles, using yarns that derive from petrochemicals, there is a particular problem. 'The challenge is that because of the critical situations which these fabrics go into, they have to be robust. We can't just say, "Take that one: we're not sure if it's good, but it's recycled." That's not going to work. But we should go back to all our products and try to produce them cleanly, even if 90% of them are mission critical.'

A tour of Arville's Wetherby mill with the head of textile production, Simon Hartley, is a fascinating experience. Simon has been a weaver since his youth; an excellent communicator, he knows and loves his job. The factory is huge and very clean. The machinery works twenty-four hours a day, Monday to Friday. Apart from the usual array of rapier looms and warping machines, Simon is keen to show me the scourer, which washes and dries the woven fabrics, and the stenter, which adds treatments to render them flame-proof, rot-proof and water-proof, stretches them to an exact width and bakes them. I ask him about the four-metre-wide fabric that is passing through. 'That's for the seats of Toyota cars,' he says. Elsewhere they are making firemen's gear, combat clothing and body armour for soldiers, tubular reinforcing fabric for engine hoses.... 'We send two containers of these each month to Romania, packed with hoses for Volvo trucks.'

Aesthetic qualities are not a priority for these textiles, but many of them are surprisingly beautiful. The aerospace samples (pictured) include two fine multifilament polyester fabrics in dark blue, a nylon in dark olive green, a natural linen, a white cotton, a black reinforced honeycomb acrylic and a camouflage fabric. The materials have science-fiction names: Twaron, Dyneema, Vectran. Perhaps the strangest of them all is Kevlar – a pale yellow colour that turns orange when exposed to light, it looks like a piece of rough plastic sacking. Simon hands me a pair of scissors. 'You'll have job to cut that,' he says. I give it a go. The scissors make no impression at all.

Kevlar was first synthesised at the DuPont Experimental Station in Delaware in 1964. It was a classic 'accidental discovery' by a company chemist, Stephanie Kwolek, who was working on a lightweight substitute for the steel cords used in car and aircraft tyres. One of her many apparently unsuccessful experiments produced a cloudy liquid, quite unlike others in appearance and consistency. She tried squirting it from a syringe. The resulting thread was unusual: it 'spun beautifully', was highly resistant to heat and five times stronger than steel. After further testing and development, the substance (chemical name poly-paraphenylene terephthalamide) was marketed as Kevlar. That was in 1971. It is used today in hundreds of applications. The chemistry of its production, however, is a complex subject. To a layman the process, requiring high temperatures and gallons of sulphuric acid, looks ripe for that prescient comment: 'we should go back to all our products and try to produce them cleanly'.

Camira

Fabrics today can be made from some improbable materials: pineapple leaves, orange skins, nettles, potatoes, old coffee grounds, yeast, even mycelium (the underground threads that connect colonies of mushrooms). These are being transformed by pioneering biotechnology companies into spinnable fibres and used by some of the world's major fashion and sports brands to create bags, shoes and clothing, with an eye to ecologically conscious consumers. At the same time, traditional plant fibres, derived from flax, hemp and jute, are finding new applications. Alongside these are initiatives like Seaqual, which collects plastic waste from the sea and transforms it into high-quality yarn. When you touch these fabrics, you would never guess their origin. The use of such yarns is one of the special characteristics of a remarkable Yorkshire company, Camira.

Camira started life in 1974, supplying fabrics for office furniture. David Hill was the man behind it, and his idea was simple: to offer a single product line, in limited colours, with next-day delivery. He called the business Camborne Fabrics, based as it was in his house on Camborne Drive, Huddersfield. The speed and efficiency of his service was unique and he was quickly successful. By 1985 he was ready to expand into production. He bought one of his suppliers, Hopton Weavers, and

A display at Camira's London showroom tells the story of its developing use of sustainable materials, from recycled polyester in 1997 to ocean plastic in 2020. Along the way are traceable wool, stinging nettles, harvested flax and closed loop (recycled yarns).

took over their mill at Mirfield with all its operations: warping, weaving, finishing, warehousing and distribution. He was soon selling overseas. In 1997 Camborne was acquired by Interface Inc, an American flooring company with a fabric division that specialised in recycled polyesters.

In 2000 Camborne's manufacturing moved to Meltham Mills in Huddersfield, which now has more than 100 looms and 400,000 square feet of floor space. Furtex Fabrics, a Halifax company specialising in plush wool velours for public transport, was added to the portfolio in 2003. In 2006 Interface decided to withdraw from the UK and sold the company to its Yorkshire management team. They renamed the business Camira – reflecting its origin in 'Camborne' as well as their hopes for a bright new era, spelt with an 'i' to avoid confusion with 'camera' – also suggesting a note of wonder, as in Latin *mirabilis* or 'admirable'. That same year, needing more space, Camira opened a factory in Lithuania, where weaving of transport fabrics, upholstery services, sampling production and polypropylene yarn manufacture are still carried out today. In 2007 they acquired John Holdsworth & Company, which specialised in upholstery fabrics for buses and trains and had supplied London Underground since 1863. In 2012 they opened a dye house, and in 2013 bought Stork Brothers, offering blending, carding and spinning of yarns. In 2019 they took over Holmfirth Dyers to expand their dyeing and finishing capabilities, adding a specialist wool recycling business, iinouiio (an acronym for 'it is never over until it is over') in 2022.

David Hill's original formula of a single product line and limited colours no longer applies – there are currently more than 2,500 fabrics and colours available, and the market has grown to include hospitality and leisure, residential furnishing, educational and healthcare environments. Still the old commitment to service holds good. The original fabric range, 'Main Line', has been expanded and improved, and it remains one of the company's best sellers.

As well as spinning, dyeing, weaving, finishing and 'cut and sew' facilities in England and Lithuania, Camira has regional sales offices in Germany and the United States. A showroom in Clerkenwell, London, provides a shopwindow in the capital: a contemporary space where visitors can handle the fabrics, talk to staff and get an immediate sense of the high level of design and ethical values of the company.

About three-quarters of Camira's worldwide trade is in furnishing fabrics, the remainder in transport. Turnover in 2024 was £80 million. Apart from its hard-earned commercial success, two aspects of the company today are particularly striking: commitment to good design, and sustainability.

Left: Camira's London showroom, which demonstrates the company's design philosophy: 'Our fabrics bring interiors to life. They bring colour, texture, design and personality to the interiors they furnish. They're the first thing we see, so they set the tone and create the mood.'

Below: The design studio at Camira's head office in Mirfield, West Yorkshire (2025).

The design department at Mirfield feels more like an art college than a workplace: spacious, airy, with large work surfaces, mood-boards, and a team of designers at work among piles of magazine cuttings, fabric samples, sketches and gatherings from the woods and fields. A quiet but intense creative atmosphere prevails. I ask one of the senior designers, Hayley Barrett, about her work. We stand at the 'colour and trend wall', which she describes as the focal point of the department, where ideas are gathered. Evolving with the seasons, it acts as a source of inspiration and colour influences, a reminder of the aesthetic effects they are trying to achieve.

A graduate of Huddersfield University, with a BSc in woven textile design, Hayley worked for a company supplying Marks & Spencer, Mothercare and major fashion brands for fifteen years before joining Camira in 2007. She explains the way designers work, taking into account a range of considerations: function, cost, recommended materials, the brief from the customer, perhaps a colour palette provided by an architect or interior designer, as well as trends in colour, fashion and society. 'We've noticed that the workplace is becoming more hybrid, it's becoming a softer-feeling kind of place, more reflecting the residential. This is particularly since COVID. It's a space where you don't notice the passing of time, you're not clock-watching, you're actually comfortable in your environment. Colours are a huge part of that. As is texture. We're seeing a lot more of this and it's continuing: more sofa-style, breakout areas. Mobile technology has played a huge part, because young people are more used to working on laptops and wandering around, not necessarily sitting at a desk. So therefore the colours, the textures, the style of the sofas, all the little zones, the little pods, reflect that change of work style.'[36]

Hayley speaks proudly of the many Design Guild awards that the team has received. When asked about competing with cheaper imports from abroad, she says with calm assurance, 'At the lower end, where you're looking at big volume products, there is always the temptation – and the threat, if you like – of being able to get that product cheaper elsewhere. But one of our best-selling polyesters started life as a product bought cheaper from overseas. It needed improving, so we took it in-house; we were able to develop it and be more efficient in production, and it's one of our best sellers now. It's not always the easiest way to go to the other side of the world. There are price and currency fluctuations, things you can't control, like everything that's going on at the moment with American tariffs, there are customs duties, conflicts – and all of a sudden it takes you twice as long to get a container from one side of the world to the other.'

Camira's customers, she says, are appreciative of what a British manufacturer can do. 'They know they can come to us if they want a particular colour and they want it quick – and they want a conversation with somebody who knows how to interpret what they say: "I want something bluer, slightly thinner, slightly fuller in colour..." There are things other than price that are harder to measure: our experience and knowledge for example, particularly with wool and bast fibres [made from plant stems] where we are way ahead of everybody else.'

Two junior designers have interesting stories of their own. Nicola Costello, who has a degree in classical music as well as one in textile design, received a student award from the Worshipful Company of Weavers and found her first job through the Entry to Work Scheme, which she described as 'incredibly helpful at a difficult time, a real vote of confidence'. We discuss the design project that she is working on. This involves studying the colours of two Camira fabrics made with Seaqual yarn – Oceanic and Quest. These are made with significant amounts of ocean plastic, so the ethical credentials are good, but she has been given the task of expanding the colour palette, particularly for the transport industry. She is doing this through trend research, exploration of 'colour friendship groups', comparisons with other fabrics in the collection and experiments at the dye house. Her approach is a combination of thoroughness and openness to new stimuli – both a laboratory scientist and a creative designer.

Another beneficiary of a Worshipful Company of Weavers' grant is Rebecca Brogden. Having studied at Kidderminster Academy, she was working for Hield furnishing fabrics in Huddersfield when her employers nominated her for a Young Designers Award in 2006. When she won, she took a trip to study colour and architecture in Barcelona. At Camira she is engaged in sourcing – 'finding fabrics that we can't make ourselves'– so as to add to the company's hospitality range. This involves research at trade fairs and online, liaising with other mills around the world, seeking out suppliers that are 'like-minded in creativity and sustainability'. Camira may use the fabric as it is or colour it, but buying-in is a much quicker process than developing a new product from scratch.

She also sources fabrics for Camira's sister company in the United States, Luna. When I ask if this has different criteria from buying for the UK, she lists from memory a host of divergent regulations and codes for chemical treatments, abrasion-resistance, flame-retardancy and 'bleach cleanability' (that is, colour-fastness after repeated cleaning with a 10 per cent bleach solution) –yet another part of the design brief that the average occupant of a sofa would never begin to

Camira's ReSKU 2.0 fabric, which is woven from recycled waste yarn.

suspect. Rebecca has been with Camira for six months. Soon she will move on to weave design.

After my conversation about sustainability at Arville Textiles, I am a little more wary of the claims that companies make in this complex area, where every trick of the copywriter's art is deployed to make heavy polluters sound like agents of Greenpeace. Still, the commitment to use yarns made of recycled wool, or plastic reclaimed from the world's seas, is surely a step in the right direction.[37]

Camira started on this path fifty years ago – at first without acknowledging the recycled elements in their cloth. Later, as fashionable opinion caught up, they realised that this was a prime selling feature. They recycled the wool from army jumpers to produce a fabric that they called ReSKU. That was in 1998. The latest version is ReSKU 2.0, developed at their iinouiio wool recycling plant in Huddersfield to celebrate the company's fiftieth birthday. Alan Williams, Camira's chief executive officer, describes how it's made: 'We take all of our yarn waste from the transport fabrics that we weave in Lithuania. We rip them back to fibres, make a new yarn and weave it into this. We don't dye it. We sort the colours of the waste yarn into piles so we don't have to dye it again, we're reusing the original colours. This is 79% of our waste coming into it, and the remaining 21% is flax, a natural fibre which gives it inherent flame retardancy.'[38]

The aesthetic of ReSKU 2.0, with its basket-like hopsack weave, is described as 'naturally homespun'. It comes in twenty-four colourways reminiscent of natural scenes: autumn woods, rough sea, cloud-dappled hills, rocky screes. It proved an instant winner with one of Britain's major banks, whose designers said, 'We love this so much, and the story behind it. We're going to make this fit within our corporate colours. We don't want you to change it.'

'That,' says Alan Williams, 'was unheard of, because in the past they would always ask, "Can you match this? Can you match that?" But this time they just said they would buy it as it is.'

Four stages in the making of Camira's ReSKU 2.0 fabrics, from yarn waste to furnishing fabric.

CHAPTER 4

Artist Weavers

To let threads be articulate again and find a form for themselves ... not to be sat on, walked on, only to be looked at, is the raison d'être of my pictorial weavings.[39]

In the 1940s, while teaching at Black Mountain College in the United States, the German weaver Anni Albers began to make what she referred to as 'pictorial weavings'. Her creative journey had begun in the Bauhaus weaving studios in 1922, one of only two studios, alongside ceramics, thought suitable for women students in this pioneering arts educational establishment. When Hitler came to power in 1933, Anni Albers and her husband Josef left for America, where they were offered jobs teaching art. Their influence was enormous: Josef as a painter and colour theorist, Anni as a weaver. A significant exponent of Modernist abstraction, Anni was given a solo show at New York's Museum of Modern Art (MoMA) in 1949, the first dedicated to a weaver.

Above: Anni Albers (born Annelise Elsa Frieda Fleischmann; 1899–1994) photographed in 1935 by her husband Josef Albers.

Left: Anni Albers, *La Luz 1* (1947), linen and metallic thread (47 cm × 82.5 cm), made to be framed and hung on the wall, was inspired by a trip to Mexico taken with her artist husband, Josef Albers. Irregular in its weave structure and unstable both in texture and colour, it is the antithesis of a useful fabric. Through its myriad minute shifts and jumps, through the material embodiment in thread of its maker's journey of thought, emotion and memory, it becomes a moving evocation of mood, history, architecture, landscape and light.

Although she was little known to the public in Britain until an exhibition at the Tate in London in 2019, Albers's insight into the expressive potential of weave directly or indirectly inspired the work of the artists we will consider in this chapter.

Of course there had been textile art before 1947. Albers herself credits the ancient weavers of Peru as her masters, whose excavated fragments still retain 'the magic of things not yet found useful'.[40] In medieval Europe, woven tapestries were considered the acme of artistic expression and priced accordingly.[41] These were created by anonymous craftsmen and women, interpreting cartoons provided by some of the leading artists of the era. But, as Albers saw it, subsequent industrialisation of the weaving process had so accustomed human beings to seeing woven materials as useful that they were no longer seen as something 'in itself fulfilled'.[42] As the twentieth century dawned, however, a new spirit was abroad. Rigid distinctions between the strictly functional, the purely decorative and fine art were challenged.[43] And for many – including Albers and her mentor at the Bauhaus, Gunta Stölzl – the pliable grid of woven textile provided as forceful a metaphor for the reordering of civilisation as the austere geometries of Modernist architecture or the cubist experiments of Picasso and Braque.

In Britain, the idea of weaving as art had been revived in the 1870s by the Arts and Crafts movement. This was a nostalgic, historically informed attempt to champion hand craft against mechanised industrial manufacture. Its leader, William Morris, was so inspired by medieval precedent that he taught himself tapestry weaving in 1877, before establishing commercial studios in Queen Square, London and at Merton Abbey.

At about the time of the First World War (1914–18), a more forward-looking, modernist spirit began to stir among British weavers. Ethel Mairet (1872–1952) set up her first hand-weaving classes in 1913, believing that the craft could be as useful to industry as it could be to art. Indeed, the closer allied to an art discipline it became, the better it could serve the new technologies. She was a strong admirer of what she called Professor Gropius's forward-looking 'creative idea', as founder and first director of the Bauhaus, to gather together in one school 'all sides of knowledge needed for the production of a fundamental artist–worker–thinker–human being'.[44] She even persuaded Gunta Stölzl to write an account of the Bauhaus education system for English readers, thus acknowledging the global significance of the school's progressive ideas despite its closure in 1933. As it happened, during the 1930s, it was above all the more commercial sector of textile design that flourished in the United Kingdom, encouraged by new customs duties to protect British manufacture during the global slump; but Mairet's ideas would later bear fruit in many different contexts.

The 'Acanthus and Vine' tapestry, woven wool, with some silk, on a cotton warp, 191 (max.) × 234 cm, at Kelmscott Manor, Oxfordshire, the home of William Morris. Designed and worked by Morris in 1879, this was his first attempt at tapestry. He had the loom installed in his bedroom at Kelmscott and taught himself to weave this particular type of French 'Verdure' tapestry. Apparently, it took him 516 hours.

Peter Collingwood

After the Second World War, as part of the creative explosion in art and design ignited by the 1951 Festival of Britain, weaving once more became an experimental medium. A key figure here was Peter Collingwood (1922–2008). While training as a doctor, Collingwood came upon a loom in a hospital's occupational therapy department: 'At the time, I knew absolutely nothing about weaving; all I saw was a machine.'[45] He spent two years in the army doing national service, taking with him a portable hand-made loom. He then switched career. His first step was to spend six weeks with Ethel Mairet in Ditchling, to learn properly how to hand weave, an experience he described as 'an eye-opener because it was the first time I had met somebody who you'd now say was weaving art fabrics'.[46] He set up a rug-making workshop in north London, in 1953, where he built his own equipment. From 1957 Collingwood became a close friend of the potter Hans Coper, through their association with the Digswell Arts Trust in Hertfordshire. At Digswell, Collingwood developed methods of shaft-shifting to enable complex geometric designs, some involving weaving at an angle, a technique he called 'anglefells'. Indeed, technique was Collingwood's primary source of inspiration. He once said: 'I try to exploit what a technique will give me rather than impose a design on a technique.'

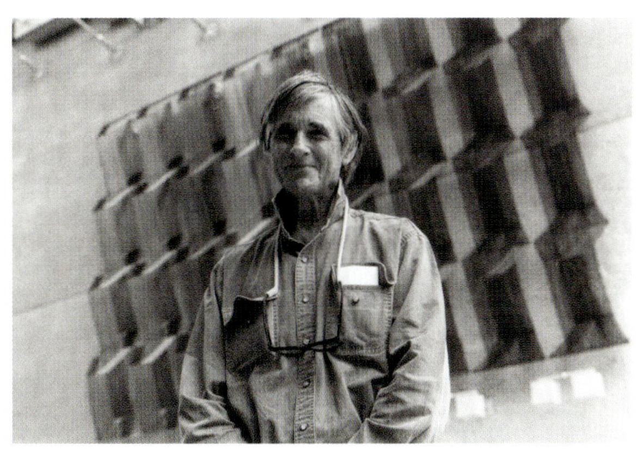

Peter Collingwood in front of his Steelweave, made using his macrogauze techniques from stainless steel fibre, at Kiryu Performing Arts Centre, Japan, 1977.

Collingwood is best known for his distinctive 'Macrogauze' wall-hangings, made by crossing warps over one another in zigzag and sideways patterns. The first of these, Macrogauze 1, was created in 1964, combining steel and brass with linen threadwork. It was exhibited in the Victoria and Albert Museum's touring exhibition *Weaving for Walls* between 1965 and 1967, a show that championed a fine art approach to weave. Through his many works and publications, Collingwood has had an enduring impact on subsequent generations of makers.

PETER COLLINGWOOD
MACROGAUZE WALL HANGINGS

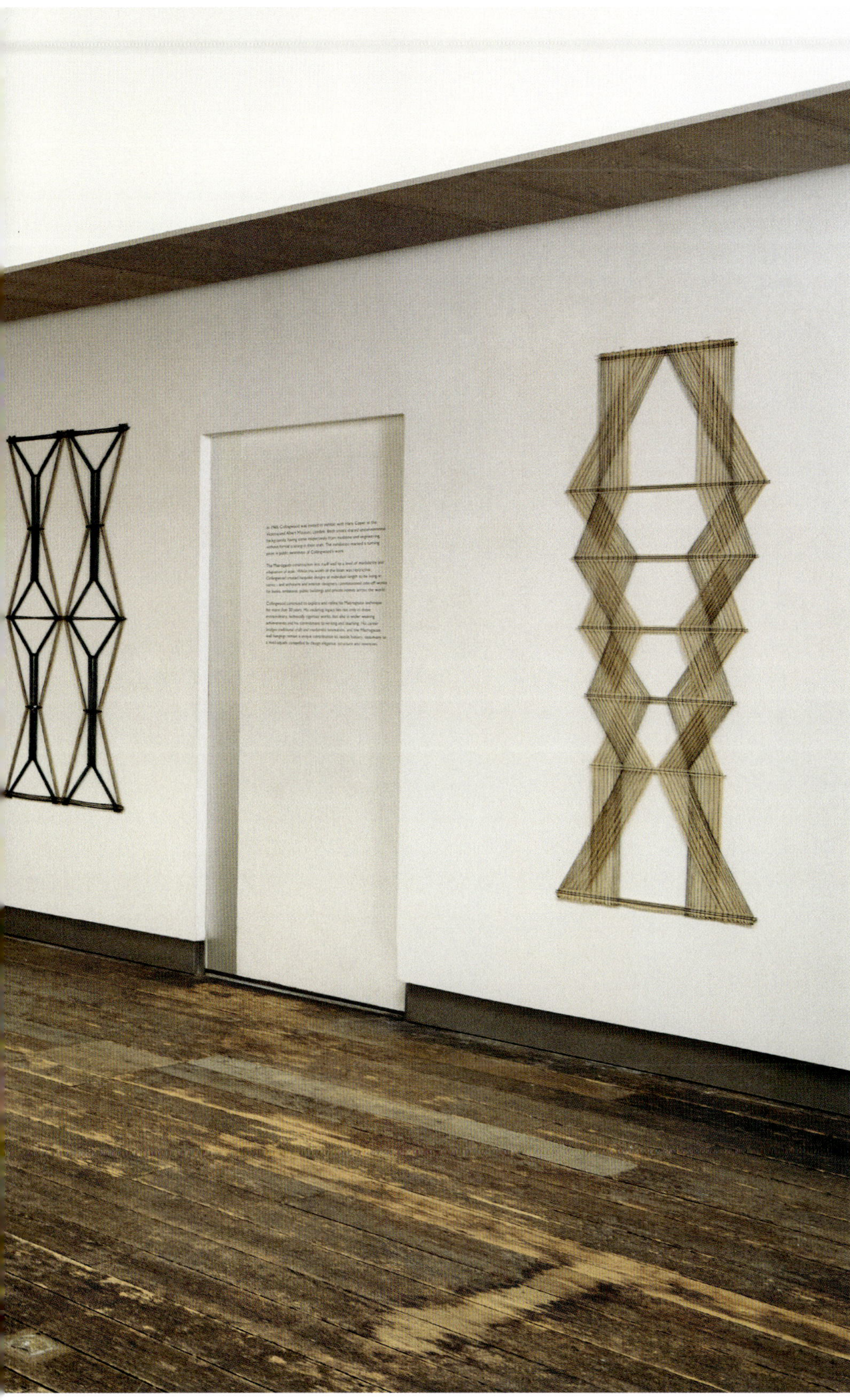

Collingwood's own largely monochromatic weaves share Hans Coper's palette and analytical approach to form, colour and texture. Here a selection is displayed at Margaret Howell's shop on Wigmore Street in London as part of the exhibition 'Peter Collingwood: Macrogauze wall hangings' (2025).

Ann Sutton

In 1987, Collingwood reflected, 'Designing is difficult. We're not living in a tradition, are we?'[47] Ann Sutton (born in 1935) had no such inhibitions. As Diane Sheehan noted in her essay for the Crafts Council's exhibition of Sutton's work in 2003, 'Clarity, boldness, wit and logic are the most apparent and enduring hallmarks of Ann Sutton's work.'[48] Refusing to be restricted by history, purpose, process or even material, her work, which she is still producing, has ranged freely across scale and kind of object – from woven chairs and three-dimensional woven sculptures, to industrially produced bedcovers and large-scale wall hangings, to miniature textiles and woven and

Above: Ann Sutton 5 × 5 = 25 (1977), rayon, lurex and nylon monofilament, 216 cm × 167 cm. Made to commemorate the Silver Jubilee of Queen Elizabeth II and exhibited by the British Crafts Council. Many pieces bear the description 'own technique', underlining the experimental nature of Sutton's approach – whether that is her method of darning brightly coloured knitted and Dacron-stuffed tubes into squares which are then sewn together, or her use of the complicated mathematics of pendulum permutations to govern her colour choices and weave structures.

Ann Sutton Primary Unit Cube and Primary Unit Square 1979. These loom-woven miniatures were exhibited at the Fourth International Biennial of Miniature Textiles at the British Crafts Council.

painted-over artworks. As she said in 1986, 'I work in the technique of weaving, sometimes as an artist, sometimes as a designer, sometimes as a craftsperson. I would starve if I just concentrated on fine art, so I am doing all three and I find they complement each other.'[49]

Sutton has been adventurous too in accessing every available technology – from pencil or knitting needle to hi-tech power-looms – and many different materials from linen to new fibres and old industrial materials like extruded fluorescent filaments and stainless steel.

Underlying all, there is what Sheehan refers to as 'weave-thinking'. Sutton's designs are governed not by aesthetics but by the same fundamental binary over/under, positive/negative dualities that govern computer programming. It is little surprise to learn that Sutton joined the Computer Art Society in 1968 and was an early adopter of computer-aided technology in the 1980s. Her most successful works satisfy above all through their marriage of concept and realisation: 'I am deeply suspicious of Beauty,' Sutton says, 'but often when I get the material/structure right, beauty appears, often in unconventional ways'.[50]

Born in Stoke-on-Trent, to a family that 'had worked in the pottery industry for aeons', Sutton came to weaving circuitously, via a pottery course at Cardiff College of Art. Discovering she did not enjoy wet clay beneath her finger nails, she moved to embroidery, before, in her final year, a requirement to take a course in another area led her to weave. The emphasis was on designing for industry, with the teacher 'eschewing all ideas of hand-spinning, vegetable dyeing etc,' Sutton remembers. 'I loved it... the medium was dry and countable.' Graduating in 1956, she worked as both artist and teacher – first at West Sussex College of Art and then at Croydon Technical College under the designer Enid Marx. Experience studying tapestry, basic design and construction at the Glamorgan Summer School, in Barry, South Wales in the early 1960s was transformative. The Summer School, heavily influenced by Bauhaus ideas, encouraged interaction between students of crafts, fine art, music and language, and introduced Sutton to post-war art movements such as the Art Textile movement of the 1960s. As well as exploring fundamentals of colour and space, she met the constructivist artists Kenneth and Mary Martin. When her own course was cancelled, Sutton took a course with Kenneth Martin, 'TO BE ASTOUNDED that he was describing an attitude to work, a way of thinking, that had only recently occurred to me as appropriate for the woven textile.' With inspiration drawn from geometry rather than nature, and with a dedication to machine construction rather than hand carving, Constructivism offered Sutton a contemporary philosophy of art that suited her approach to her medium. Only much later did she learn that the Martins had been weavers first. A prolific writer and active educator, Sutton in turn has inspired many others.

It has taken many years for the conceptual and expressive power of textiles to be fully acknowledged. Since the 2019 Anni Albers exhibition in London, however, there have been many full-scale textile exhibitions at major public art galleries. While twenty-four pieces of Sutton's work are in the V&A's collection, it is a mark of a new era that in 2021 Tate purchased three works by Sutton for their permanent collection.

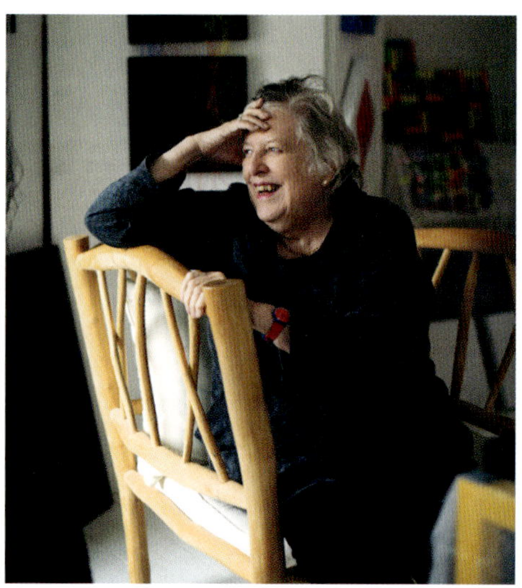

Mary Restieaux

Mary Restieaux, born in 1945, represents an almost opposite strand within art textiles. Where Sutton is focused on structure,[51] Restieaux has been a leading figure within the revival of ikat (a South Asian tie-dyeing technique) in British weaving, with colour her pre-eminent passion. Restieaux found her way to weaving by accident. An only child growing up in rural Norfolk, with her father a carpenter and her mother a teacher, she spent a great deal of time happily alone making things. 'I sewed and sewed and sewed,' she remembers. After studying for a degree in History of Art at Cambridge College of Art and Technology, Restieaux married and moved to London. Teaching art at a school in Brent, she applied for a short summer course in textiles at Chelsea College of Art, to widen her expertise. Instead, the head of textiles offered her a place on a three-year degree course. At first Restieaux assumed she would specialise in prints, then the popular choice. But in 1969 it was weave that won her interest. It was only many years later that she discovered that she was descended from a Huguenot – many of whom were silk weavers – although her ancestor, married in St Anne's Church in Soho in 1766, was also apparently a teacher of art. She moved on to the Royal College of Art in 1972, where she was taught by Marianne Straub, one of the leading commercial designers of textiles in Britain. Straub was 'brilliant', Restieaux remembers, and generous with her time.

But Straub was focused on technique and design for industry, whereas Restieaux discovered a passion for colour, dyeing and hand-weaving: 'I started dip-dyeing my warps.' A tutor suggested she look at ikat and that became her focus: 'My interest was in doing very fine work in silk.' To this day, that is what she has done.

On graduation, Restieaux continued to research and teach weaving at the Royal College of Art, creating small experimental ikat pieces that she would frame. At this point her primary ambition was not to make art; she took her designs to the fashion houses in Paris, selling ikats as samples alongside tweeds and very fine silks, which she wove in her studio on a large dobby loom. This period coincided with the founding of the Crafts Council, set up in 1971 under Lord Eccles to advise 'on the needs of the artist craftsman and to promote a nationwide interest and improvement in their products'.[52] In 1979 Restieaux was selected for the Council's prestigious Index of Makers. Victor Margrie, the first director of the Council, pointed out the similarity between Restieaux's work and the ceramics of Elizabeth Fritsch, then beginning to be recognised as outstanding works of art. Restieaux was offered an exhibition, moved into a new studio and bought an 8-shaft countermarch Harris loom, which enabled her, throughout the 1980s, to weave large pieces for exhibition and to commission. As she puts it, 'I had been calling my works scarves but then I realised they were really wall hangings.' From then on she combined making art pieces with her commercial work.

Her love of colour, expressed in her ikat pieces, led to her becoming the colour consultant for many fashion houses, including Hervé Léger, Paris, with whom she collaborated closely between 1991 and 1998, pre-eminently on his striped 'bandage' dresses. She also joined the First Eleven Studio, run by Jenny Frean RDI,[53] as a freelance designer producing samples at first for international fashion houses and then for furniture manufacturers. The Crafts Council meanwhile exhibited her artwork internationally, including in Japan.

In 1994, after submitting her work herself, Restieaux was awarded the Traditional Technique Award from the Fourth International Textile Competition in Kyoto. In 2009, her work was exhibited alongside pots by Elizabeth Fritsch,[54] a huge accolade, showing that technical expertise

Above: The studio of Mary Restieaux, who carefully tie-dyes her yarns in jewel-like colours, then lines up a series (up to fifteen) of dense fine silk warps (between 80 and 96 threads an inch) to create a single multi-coloured warp, before weaving through the usually yellow weft to create a vivid double sided warp-dominant abstract textile (**opposite**).

need not be at the expense of expressive, artistic excellence. Meanwhile she herself has become a Royal Designer for Industry. While not a prolific maker of art pieces, she has loyal admirers, including the designer and hotelier Kit Kemp, founder and creative director of the stylish Firmdale Hotels.

It seems the balance of teaching, designing and making has served Restieaux well. 'I have had the most wonderful life,' she says. It has also served to inspire many others, as those who were lucky enough to gain a scholarship administered by Restieaux or attend Restieaux's legendary annual study days in her own home studio testify.

Ptolemy Mann

Ptolemy Mann, whose intensely coloured textile artworks have long been sought after both for corporate commissions and by private collectors, openly acknowledges Restieaux's influence. In Mann's first year as a student at Central Saint Martins College of Art, Restieaux invited a group to her home to demonstrate ikat. Mann recalls, 'If you imagine what St Martins was like in the 1990s, it was all about minimalism, there was no colour. It had to be wire monofilament, it had to glow in the dark, it had to be technical somehow, it was all about innovation. I was doing plain weave, in cotton, and I was hand dyeing, and no one was interested. My aesthetic was actually closer to Mary's because I was interested in colour and geometry and that sort of Bauhaus philosophy of art-making.'[55]

Mann, who was born in New York City in 1972, was brought up in Cranbrook, England, by her father, a writer and astrologer, who also painted mandalas. Her mother, whom she met again when she was seventeen, was a documentary film maker based in New York. Art was all around her as a child. She enrolled on the textile design course at Central Saint Martins, after a tutor on her Maidstone Art College Foundation Course had said: 'You are a terrible painter, but you are a girl, and you are good with colour, so why don't you go off to do textiles?'[56] When she arrived, Central Saint Martins (still in its Charing Cross Road headquarters) was in its heyday: 'Alexander McQueen had just left, Stella McCartney was in my year. It was a really exciting moment.' More important for Mann was that Garth Lewis, painter and educator, was still teaching colour theory one day a week for the whole of the first year, according to the legendary Bauhaus curriculum developed by Johannes Itten, Paul Klee, Wassily Kandinsky and Josef Albers. Mann recalls, 'You would paint a hundred squares between blue and orange, you would do a value

Ptolemy Mann, Alqa Orange, 2023.

Ptolemy Mann, 'After Aalto' (Orange Gold Green), 2021. This is one of three panels, all 120 cm × 80 cm, inspired, according to Ptolemy Mann, 'by the colour palette developed by the artist Eino Kauria with Alvar Aalto for The Paimio Sanatorium, which was completed in 1933'.

chart, a chroma chart. It was all about the interaction of colour and mixing colour, so it was phenomenal.'

The fact that Central Saint Martins only provided white and black yarn, so you had to learn to dye, confirmed Mann in her path. In her third year, as others considered jobs in industry, fashion, interiors or colour trend prediction, she maintained her commitment to making art, deepening her understanding of colour and plain weave technique. She says, 'I think I was always very practical about it. But I did know I wanted to make non-functional textiles.' At the time that was a brave choice 'because it is a very different career path for any artist, but choosing a craft-based medium to do that, especially 30 years ago, that was a risky decision'.

Fortunately, in her first vacation at the Royal College of Art, in 1996, she won a commission from KPMG to create an artwork for the lobby of one of their buildings in the city. It consisted of seven hangings, representing seven countries. 'I learned so much through doing that project... [including]... how I, as an abstract weaver, could interpret something as complex as the idea of national identity,' she recalls. It was through this project that Mann realised also that she no longer wanted to create loose hangings: 'there was this problem of the void behind the back which really bothered me. And even at that point my work was very linear.' As she explains, 'Unlike other weavers, when I was weaving the cloth, it was under tight tension. Most weavers love the moment when you cut the cloth off and I always hated that moment because you lost the tension. Those beautiful lines disappeared and lost their integrity.' So despite the disapproval of her head of department, Mann began to stretch her weaves, once finished, over frames, as if they were canvases. She has stretched every artwork since. One incidental benefit is that her immaculate weaves do not need to be framed. Looking at them from afar, with their thrilling intensity of colour, you could mistake them for paintings; there is so little of the hand-made aesthetic about them. On the other hand, the particular precise dynamism of vertical lines, like a hectic graph, where two contrasting colours meet, is only achievable through thread, a source of wonder as you come close.

For decades Mann has earned her living making to commission intensely coloured abstract art textiles on a grand, often architectural, scale. Her reference points have been painters rather than weavers, American artists like Donald Judd, James Turrell, Barnett Newman, Mark Rothko and the Abstract Expressionists. For exhibitions and private commissions, she has executed myriad smaller pieces, sometimes creating several works on a single long warp, experimenting as she goes with colour according to her mood.[57]

Recently, Mann has taken her art in a radically new direction. As her first marriage crumbled and it became clear that she would never have children, she suddenly felt a surge of creative energy. One morning, she woke, determined to paint one hundred works that same day. She says: 'From 1997 when I set up my studio to 2018, 21 years, I didn't touch paint. I was very devoted to weaving. It never crossed my mind to not make art through weaving.' That day she made sixty-seven small paintings. 'They are the complete opposite of the weaving: they are quick, gestural, immediate. They come from the gut, from the heart. Weaving is so cerebral. It was magical.' Excited, she made more and more, developing a whole separate art practice of liquid watercolour pigments or acrylic gouache on wet black and white watercolour paper. Her inspirations are the American colour-field painter Helen Frankenthaler and the English master of colour, painter Howard Hodgkin. Mann says, 'I use Arches paper which is 100% cotton, cold pressed paper. There is something about the luminosity of colour on this paper, which connects with the weaving.'

During lockdown, these works began to sell well. But then another possibility opened up: 'I asked myself, what if I painted on top of the weaving?' In some ways, this seems entirely logical – after all, what is a canvas if not a woven textile? On the other, to paint on a weave is a radical action. Ann Sutton had painted on some of her weaves in the 1980s and 1990s: 'I needed to be able to quell the textile character without losing the weave structure,' Sutton explains.[58] Sutton notes with amusement: 'The work was taken more seriously by some, now that it included PAINT. And it annoyed some purists, which I liked. Handweaving is a sacred area.' Mann too feels the enormous tension of breaking a taboo: 'Weaving is all about keeping everything dry. Now here I am with this loaded paint brush (I don't use a palette) and I just put the paint directly onto the weaving and I move it around.' The results are startling, introducing a different three-dimensional quality to the original weavings and a subtle contrast between the calm, rigidly structured, labour-intensive coloured ground and the spontaneous, free application of the colour. Mann does not paint on all her weaves, recognising that some have a quiet intensity that does not require paint. The whole process is still evolving. But Mann is thrilled to embark on this new phase.[59]

A 3D woven structure
by Philippa Brock.

Philippa Brock

Philippa Brock has built her research and industry career from a passionate interest in three-dimensional woven fabrics. Out of this interest have sprung all strands of her career – designing for industry, teaching, curating, consulting, exhibiting and her own research-based experimental artworks. They have all been intertwined, as Brock's artworks emerge from her knowledge of the capabilities of the Jacquard power loom and her desire continually to disrupt digital loom technologies.

Brock began her professional life as a nurse. In the 1980s she took advantage of a rule allowing those who had worked for three years in the profession to take a degree in a different subject, with fees and maintenance paid. Having always sewed and made things as a child, she took a BTech at Chelsea College of Art. This led her to the BA (Hons) in Art Textiles at Goldsmiths, under a series of inspiring teachers, including Audrey Walker and Michael Brennand-Wood. Here she focused mainly on print and embroidery: 'but I wanted to learn more about weave,' she says. 'Rather than putting the imagery onto the cloth, I wanted it to be part of the cloth structure.' She applied for an MA at the Royal College of Art, where her arrival coincided with the early days of computer-aided design. Brock remembers that early on, with the RCA's old punch-card Jacquard loom, she would work out the peg plan on the computer and then revert to analogue at the loom, cutting and lacing her own Jacquard cards. But it was the potential of the digital power loom that really excited her. In 1992, Brock won a travel scholarship, which she used to go to Huddersfield where the university had an industrial digital Dataweave power Jacquard loom, enabling weavers to produce highly complex designs very rapidly in large samples. As throughout history, once again cloth manufacture was in the vanguard technologically, inventing the tools, this time digital, to serve its needs. Douglas Bland taught her how to use the software: 'And I then started this whole personal research investigation into what I could achieve. I introduced different fibres, designs and different weave structures. The technicians would sit there saying, "You can't do that Philippa." And I would say, "Watch me."'[60] Brock used Adobe Photoshop to create digital files in a format compatible with industrial power looms, increasing her ability to innovate. After graduating, she took this boundary-pushing expertise to Belgium, working with Sophis Systems N.V. and then freelance as a textile designer.

In 1994 a senior research post at Winchester School of Art gave Brock access to a new power loom, where she was able to continue her experiments into 2D and 3D woven fabrics and work with industry, including Lurex, Talbot and the Taiwan Textile Federation. During the 1990s Brock began a collaboration with Gainsborough Silk Weaving Company, weaving her own research work on one of their digital Jacquard looms. Here she continued to develop her innovative 'self-forming' fabrics, which, while flat when tensioned on the loom, gradually 'move and mould' once off the loom. A combination of specialist yarns, design and carefully constructed weave structures minimises the need for post-weaving cloth-finishing, including ironing, printing and embroidery, saving up to 40 per cent of water and energy use. From

Above: Philippa Brock. This work is an example of 'self-assembly'. The fabric appears to be two dimensional on the loom but 'self-assembles' into three dimensions when taken off the loom. For Brock, this offers an analogy to the self-assembly organisation of the tobacco mosaic virus, which was the research focus of Aaron Klug, the Nobel-prize-winning British chemist and biophysicist, with whom she collaborated on the Nobel Textiles 'Fabrics of Life' Project (2007–9). The role of these fabrics is less to be used than to visualise scientific discovery. Their mesmerising complexity communicates the intricacy of dynamic biological architecture.

Left: Philippa Brock, X-Form 2.

2000 until 2023, Brock combined this work with her academic roles, initially working at Chelsea College of Art and Design running digital textile design and subsequently managing the Woven Textile Department at Central Saint Martins.

One significant creative milestone was the Nobel Textiles 'Fabrics of Life' Project (2007–9) supported by the Medical Research Council and Epigenome Network of Excellence (NoE), involving six artist-designers working with Nobel Laureates. Brock collaborated with the British chemist and biophysicist Aaron Klug, using textile to illuminate Klug's 1982 Nobel prize-winning work on the crystal structures of protein-nucleic acid complexes. Brock was especially intrigued by the self-assembly organisation of the tobacco mosaic virus, with its arrangement of protein subunits in a helix around a ribonucleic acid (RNA) core. By analogy,

Brock designed her Self-Assembly series of fabrics to 'self assemble' as they come off the loom.

In 2012 Brock was given her first solo show, '2D–3D', at the Montreal Centre for Contemporary Textiles. For this she developed her 3D, × Form series, which explored inherently smart yarns, including fluorescent, phosphorescent and solar reactive. Since then she has exhibited widely in Canada, Asia and North America and is a member of the European Textile Network. Brock explains, 'Initially I was better known for my art practice in these territories than in the UK. I felt they valued it more highly at the time.' In 2014, however, the Worshipful Company of Weavers awarded her their prestigious Silver Medal. Besides her own artistry and commitment to teaching at university level, this recognised Brock's generous mentoring and sharing of skills and information, through her website, The Weave Shed, and her outreach and social engagement projects in Tower Hamlets. These include visionary initiatives such as The Experimental Weave Lab (with Elizabeth Ashdown), 'Weaving Futures' at London Transport Museum and being a sustainability mentor for government-funded projects with British weaving companies Dash & Miller, Tibor, and ReWeave.

Ismini Samanidou

The daughter and granddaughter of medics, Ismini Samanidou grew up in Athens with a love of mathematics, but also of working with her hands. A career in science was an obvious option, but she also had a highly developed interest in photography. This led her to take a foundation in art and design in England, where colours and textiles drew her attention. Choosing a BA in textiles at Central Saint Martins (1996–9), she was able to pursue her fascination with weave technology: 'In my third year I became particularly interested in weaving layers. I realised that if you wove three different cloths at the same time on the loom then when you take them off the loom, you can open them, and whatever you have woven flat

Ismini
Samanidou.

can become something which is three-dimensional.'[61] Although this was a design degree, 'I was making these more sculptural pieces. They even had fibre optics and wire.' With her head full of ideas, 'I did not have a plan for what I was going to become, I was just deeply involved with making.'

Winning a place on the MA course in textiles at the Royal College of Art (2001–3), Samanidou became further entranced by the capabilities of the power loom: 'What I loved about the Jacquard was the contrast between working on the hand loom, which is very slow and controlled, and this large industrial machine, which was very loud and very fast.' Samanidou would stand beside the technician and ask him to stop the loom and change the thread: 'It was almost like choreography, you could see something emerging really quickly.' Each piece is a one-off creation. When asked by her tutor, 'What is it?', she had no answer. 'I was interested in a certain structure, or surface or effect, not what its function was to be.'[62]

Because her way of working required an industrial loom, Samanidou accepted a post as artist in residence at Falmouth College of Art in 2005. They had just

THE WEAVER'S TRADE

From photography to textile handweaving. Samanidou's interest in textures and surfaces has led her to use a variety of techniques, including stitching, embroidery and over-printing. Other projects involve corrosives, such as devore paste, used to restructure or emboss fabric by selectively destroying different fibres.

acquired a power loom and Samanidou was sent to Galashiels for training with ScotWeave, so that she could work as the technician with the students but also on her own projects. Besides some commercial design work for the high-end fabric and wallpaper companies Christopher Farr and George Spencer Designs, she began to get private, public and corporate art commissions. Because of the loom, she could work at scale. The first, a wall-hanging, from the Worshipful Company of Weavers, was the first wall-hanging they had commissioned to be made on a Jacquard loom. 'Because it was made on a digital loom they were asking, "Is it art? Is it craft?"' It is now part of the V&A's collection. During her time at Falmouth, Samanidou worked with a research group called 'autonomatic', organised by the ceramicist, Dr Katie Bunnell. 'It was all about the interface between the digital and craft, the hand and the machine.' Samanidou collaborated with a woodworker

Opposite: A weave by Ismini Samanidou using paper thread.

Below: Ismini Samanidou in Bangladesh: 'Weave is a way to time travel – you can feel part of a different time, because you can learn how textiles were made in the past. It is a language, so anywhere in the world you can connect with people; and it is a huge lesson that things need time to be made.'

Timeline by Ismini Samanidou, shortlisted for the Jerwood Contemporary Makers Prize in 2009.

called Garry Allson, translating weave structures on to wood via a milling machine. She was invited on residencies abroad – to Sarawak to research the different types of making, and then to Bangladesh for the British Council's Silk Route Project, where she both taught design and researched different styles of weaving for ten weeks. 'There was this hi-tech research on the loom and how you can transfer digital data – which felt quite of the time – and then there was this amazing possibility to look at exquisite craft skills and techniques using very simple tools.'

After eight years, Samanidou returned to London. She began juggling teaching with her own work, which gave her access to large power looms for significant public commissions, including thirteen textiles for the National Theatre. In 2009 Samanidou was shortlisted for the Jerwood Contemporary Makers Prize. Part of what she produced was a vast double cloth sixteen metres long and three metres high, which spiralled round within the exhibition space to create a fluid textile room. It was inspired by the history of the site of the Jerwood Space in Union Street, South London and made at the Oriole Mill in Hendersonville, North Carolina, then a rare facility allowing artists access to large-scale industrial looms. Her solo show, *Topography: Recording place – mapping surface* in 2012 at the Crafts Study Centre in Farnham was further demonstration of her power to conjure the histories, atmospheres and textures of places through weave. The show travelled to the United States.

In 2014 Samanidou received an invitation to take up a residency at the Josef and Anni Albers Foundation, in Connecticut. She seized the opportunity to go back to basics, taking nothing with her but a camera, some drawing materials and her shuttles: 'I had got to the point where I thought that if I couldn't weave on a Jacquard, I couldn't weave at all. Which is of course not true.'

Since her return to England Samanidou has had a child and moved to Eastbourne. Her practice has broadened out to encompass experimental hand weaving and large-scale thread-based installation. Since 2002, Samanidou has worked a great deal with paper thread among other yarns: 'I was interested in paper because I had all these pictures of peeling walls which I was trying to replicate in textile and it felt the most appropriate material.' More recently she has worked on an installation in an old thread factory in Athens, where she has not woven the thread, but instead unravelled a 21-kilometre warp through a space to evoke the decline of this once thriving factory. Called 'How to Build a Universe', it offered the analogy of an unwoven thread and the increasingly unused skills of the declining workforce. Samanidou has found, through weave, ways to address the social, historical and economic questions that intrigue her.

Rita Párniczky

Rita Párniczky graduated in 2009. She was invited to join the Worshipful Company of Weavers in 2020, became a Freeman in 2021 and a Liveryman in 2022. Right from the beginning hers has been a determinedly artistic pathway, with drawing, photography and video distinct aspects of her work, alongside her sculptural textile practice. Párniczky came to London from Hungary to do an arts foundation course. Although her portfolio showed mostly painting, drawing and three-dimensional construction, she then chose to apply for the textiles course at Central Saint Martins. There it was weave that drew her interest: 'I wanted something that challenged me, that might be risky. If you have an empty piece of paper you are completely free, your hand can go everywhere. Whereas with weave, with a loom, there is limitation, restriction, a unique language one must master to make work.'[63]

In her second year, Párniczky began to develop an interest in the structure of the woven material, what lies beneath the surface. 'I was always curious about X-rays,

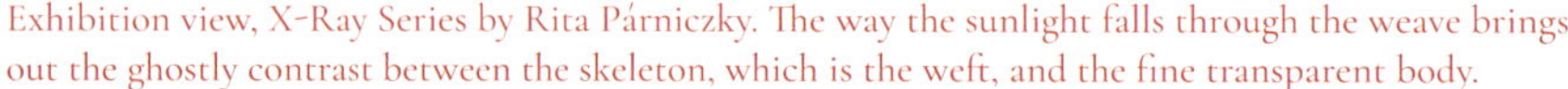

Exhibition view, X-Ray Series by Rita Párniczky. The way the sunlight falls through the weave brings out the ghostly contrast between the skeleton, which is the weft, and the fine transparent body.

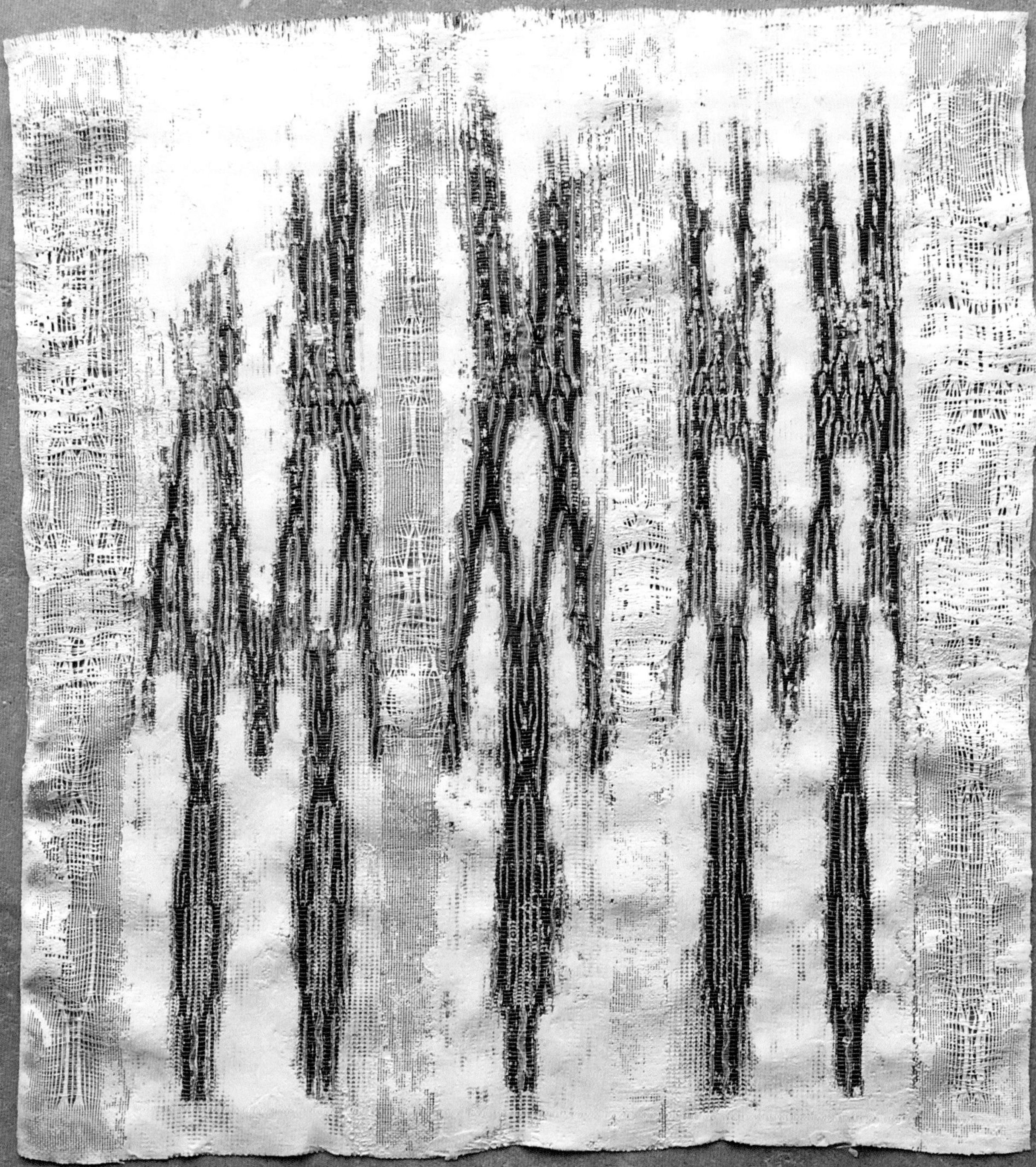

A mixed-media artwork by Rita Párniczky, from the 'Broken Bones' series.
The skeletal textile is covered in plaster, which is then rubbed away.

because you see something that otherwise you wouldn't see, something invisible to the naked eye.' She recognised the parallel between the human skeleton and the role of a warp, fundamental to the textile's construction but often hidden. Her research developed along two strands. First, she explored the use of X-rays as a source of imagery. Then, instead of using real hospital X-rays, Párniczky was encouraged by her tutors to find her own way of making imagery that could represent X-rays. Párniczky saw the potential of producing prints of unusual objects and materials, captured through the ghostly black and white photogram technique, which she was introduced to in her first year at Central Saint Martins.

In parallel, she developed on the loom an original technique of weaving using nylon monofilament for both warp and weft, sometimes interspersed with black or white cotton or rayon. This way the entire vertical structure of warp is visible – allowing you to see the 'skeleton' of the fabric, especially when light is shone through it. Further, rather than being restricted by the grid pattern dictated by warp and weft, Párniczky developed a method for shifting groups of warp threads from the vertical into a sideways movement, using the warp shafts. X-Ray series, as Párniczky refers to this body of work, is either densely or loosely woven, textural, geometrical or even architectural. All her work is monochrome to help viewers focus on the structure.

Her technique was so original and her approach so distinctive that she was commissioned on graduation to produce a textile for the Worshipful Company of Weavers. With renewed confidence, she further developed the technique she had pioneered, experimenting with a wide width Leclerc loom, which allowed the artist to scale up her work. Párniczky talks about her drive to make 'something that no one else has done. Something that adds to and develops a technique.' Over the last few years she has expanded the technique into new areas. For her 'Broken Bones' series, she covers some weaves with plaster before rubbing away. It began as a response to viewers looking for function in her weaves: 'I cover the woven work in plaster, making it quite rigid so that you can no longer wear it or put it on your sofa. I was curious about how we define textiles, how we understand objects and function.' In some works, the plaster is thick and roughly cracked and broken like a landscape. In others Párniczky has rubbed so much of the plaster away that the underlying geometric black and white patterns of the weave re-emerge with a powerful figurative resonance, like revenants. In yet others she separates out the plaster and the textile, now distorted by its burying. The plaster looks like some ancient tablet of text (textile after all contains the word 'text', and both derive from

Rita Párniczky
in her studio.

texere, the Latin for 'to weave'). The fragile textile looks as if it might have been unearthed from Tutankhamun's tomb.

While making the work, Párniczky began to question why she applies plaster. She then remembered childhood accidents when she broke her bones at a very young age. The double connotations of plaster – its use in sculpture, its use in mending bones – had come together. Other developments include her frottage works, where she uses paper and graphite to make a clear, legible, print of the weave structure of a textile she has already woven, and then her cut paper works, photography and video.

Párniczky comments: 'With much of my work there is a return for some reason to bones, to structure.' She also notes the parallel with the physical structure of the universe, which is often imagined as a curved fabric of space-time, a quite precise structure that we are only starting to understand.

Párniczky's approach to her art is deeply influenced by her sensitivity to detail and her ongoing interest in pursuing her curiosity about the world through mixed-media and weave. She is definitively optimistic: 'In a way there is no failure. Everything is an experiment, something to learn from.'

CHAPTER 5

Designer Weavers

One of the most remarkable success stories in British weaving today is the independent designers who have managed to combine art and commerce. They work and create with the freedom of artists, but collaborate with industry to see their creations produced on a large scale. Their textiles are mostly intended for practical use –clothing or furnishing – but many of the designs are so arresting and unusual, so charged with energy and presence, that they feel more like works of art. Even the humbler everyday items – cushions, scarves, towels, chair-covers – are curiously lifted out of the ordinary by the beauty and boldness of their designs, their vibrant juxtapositions of colours, and their subtle complexities of structure. These design qualities are cultivated by British schools of art, in a tradition that is now almost two centuries old.[64] It is no coincidence that every one of the designers that we discuss in this chapter is art-school trained.

Margo Selby's studio and shop, Whitstable, Kent (2025). Her 16-metre hanging, *Moon Landing*, is on the right.

Emma Sewell (left) and Harriet Wallace-Jones in a train on London's Elizabeth Line, for which they designed the seat fabric. The Elizabeth Line was opened by Queen Elizabeth II on 17 May 2022.

Wallace Sewell

Anyone who has travelled on the London Underground at a quiet time of day will certainly have seen, probably sat on and perhaps even noted with interest the fabric that covers the seats. The Piccadilly Line has a pattern that combines famous landmarks: Big Ben, Tower Bridge, the London Eye and St Paul's Cathedral. The Croydon Tramlink is a bright patchwork of green, red and grey to reflect the mixed rural/urban character of the area. The Elizabeth Line's colours of purple, silver, black and white were designed to be easily seen by the visually impaired, but they also echo the silvery blue colours associated with aviation: Heathrow Airport is one of the major stops on the line.[65] Under the relentless friction of the 1.2 billion passengers who travel on the Tube every year, the seats inevitably get worn and grimy. When they are new, however, or freshly refitted after years of use, the colours blaze with life. The cloth, known as moquette, is woven from wool by Camira Fabrics of Yorkshire designed and conceived in London by Wallace Sewell.

Wallace Sewell won their first contract with London Transport in 2007, through a public competition. Their journey began more than twenty years earlier, when Harriet Wallace-Jones and Emma Sewell met on the textile design course at St Martin's School of Art in 1985. Workshops and study programmes at the school embraced colour

Transport for London moquette seat fabrics designed by Wallace Sewell.

Pages from *2000 Colour Combinations for Graphic, Textile and Craft Designers* by the painter Garth Lewis, who taught colour theory at Central Saint Martins, inspiring a generation of designers and artists, including Harriet Wallace-Jones, Emma Sewell and Ptolemy Mann.

theory, life class and drawing, which gave students the basic tools for visual creativity. Students were taught how to dye yarns, mix colour and understand the different colour palettes and their applications. They explored printed, woven and knitted textiles before specialising in weaving in the third year.

They then both studied on a two-year MA in woven textiles at the Royal College of Art, where they were encouraged to experiment with the department's power loom by the 'very kind, patient and knowledgeable' technician Roger Lewis. He had spent years in the industry and proved an expert guide to industrial weave production and manufacturing. They began to explore ways of extending their artisanal approach to projects with UK mills. The aim was to combine craft, design and industrial production – which has remained their focus to this day.

In 1990, the year they completed their studies, Harriet and Emma faced few prospects of employment. The British economy was undergoing one of its periodic slumps, and the textile industry was suffering particularly badly. A series of lucky breaks, however, gave them the confidence to set up a studio together as independent designers. The first arose at the close of their final year at the RCA, when Harriet showed her work at the New Designers exhibition in Islington. This annual event, which gives students in design the opportunity to be seen by employers, talent scouts, design agencies, journalists and the public, was set up by Peta Levi in 1985. 'Peta was a wonderful ambassador for young designers and fledgling design businesses. She involved many captains of industry and important and relevant companies who supported students and gave awards during the exhibition, with the aim that some of them would also offer jobs.'66 Harriet was awarded a prize by the Worshipful Company of Weavers. 'I was very surprised to be selected,' she says, 'especially as the award was for £1000.' They secured a setting-up grant from the Crafts Council and rented a studio in North London. 'The Crafts Council scheme was brilliant and a lifeline for young designers: the grants would pay 50% towards machinery or equipment costs. I was able to purchase my loom with a Crafts Council grant and a generous contribution from the Worshipful Company of Weavers too.' They exhibited their collaborative work for the first time in 1992 at the Chelsea Crafts Fair, where another opportunity awaited them. A New York department store, Barneys, placed an order for scarves, and asked for more the following season. Commissions followed and they slowly built up a range of stockists globally, including the Guggenheim Museum and Liberty of London.

Wallace Sewell's lambswool 'Emmeline Pinstripe' rug, hand-knotted in Nepal.

'We had no idea what our business was going to do,' says Harriet. 'My initial idea had been to either design samples and sell them at Heimtextil, the annual trade fair in Frankfurt, or to design on our handlooms and produce fabric by the metre.'[67] It was the buyers at Barneys promising to return in January to see their spring/summer scarf collection that encouraged Harriet and Emma to continue in the same vein.

They soon fell in with the rhythms of the fashion calendar, with specific months for designing samples and showcasing their collection for each season. The first creative phase involved working up design samples on handlooms, before selecting and producing full-length pieces for their collection. After showing the collection at trade fairs in the UK and abroad, they collected orders from buyers and the production phase began at the mill. The final pieces were then delivered towards the end of the summer. This seasonal pattern of design, production and distribution enabled the business to establish itself. It is a model that continues today.

The business was now growing, but in the summer of 2000 the mill they were working with in Todmorden was flooded. The machinery was wrecked and weaving abruptly ceased. Wallace Sewell had to find a new mill to meet their orders. 'Lance and Adrian Mitchell were our knights in shining armour. They came over the hill from Lancashire, picked up all our yarn and even the warp that was on the beam ready to weave, and escorted us back to County Brook Mill, their family-run mill for over 100 years. As is so often the way, what started as a problem to solve became the start of a wonderful working relationship that has lasted 25 years and is still going strong.' In 2024 Wallace Sewell began renting the top floor of County Brook Mill for cutting, sewing and dispatch.

County Brook Mill, near Colne, Lancashire, an eighteenth-century Arkwright mill, the home of Mitchell Interflex, who have been weaving on this site since 1907.

The Wallace Sewell shop in Lloyd Baker Street, Islington, North London (2023).

Apart from the contract with Transport for London, other important projects include scarves inspired by works of art shown at exhibitions at the Tate, V&A, Dulwich Picture Gallery and the Frick in New York, recreations of Bauhaus blanket designs, international brand collaborations and commissions and retail collections.

'The business has grown since we started in 1992 – originally it was just the two of us, but we now have a team of sixteen. We regularly recruit graduates, and in return for them gaining experience and training we benefit from having fresh and exciting ideas brought to our team. Most of our team joined us as graduates, often having interned with us as students. If the fit is right for all of us, they stay for the long term and join our work family. We are committed to sharing our knowledge and expertise (and even our not-so successful experiences) with the next generation of designers, artists and makers – we have both tutored at many colleges and are still regular speakers at student conferences.'

The Wallace Sewell shop in London is a small but brilliantly colourful showcase for the work, inspiring and fun to visit. It also acts as an open space, welcoming students and the public to talks, making sessions, designer collaborations or mini-exhibitions detailing the work process.

Harriet and Emma have been working together for more than thirty years. 'We have stayed true to our core values,' says Harriet, 'design excellence, technical creativity, longevity and transparency, celebration of materials and the process of making, embracing the British textile industry.'[68] Their designs are always evolving, but a distinctive and recognisable style can be seen in everything they do: bold use of colour in blocks and stripes, strongly geometric or asymmetric patterns and visible fabric structure. Often drawing inspiration from paintings, their work displays a surge of chromatic energy that is both dynamic and disciplined.

When asked about their collaborative process, Emma Sewell says: 'Initially we would design parts of the collection separately and get each other's opinion; but then, over time, we started to design together. We each have slightly different passions when weaving. For Harriet it's very much colour and proportion, for me it's structure. I think we also have different approaches to designing. I tend to have a design concept in my head, whereas Harriet very much designs at the loom using the warp as a canvas. So we come at weaving from different angles, but we're very very connected by our interest and love of colour.'

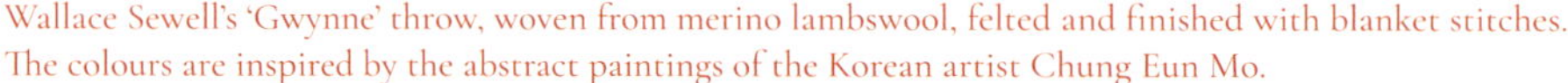

Wallace Sewell's 'Gwynne' throw, woven from merino lambswool, felted and finished with blanket stitches. The colours are inspired by the abstract paintings of the Korean artist Chung Eun Mo.

Dash & Miller

Juliet Bailey and Franki Brewer started their textile design consultancy in 2009. They had met the year before while working for a textile design consultancy in London. Before that Franki had worked for Roger Oates, the specialist in flat-weave carpets, and Juliet had done a spell for export silk weavers Bharat Silks in Bangalore, and had interned for the couture firms Malhia Kent in Paris and Jakob Schlaepfer in St Gallen – both specialists in extravagantly inventive fabric design. From these varied experiences Juliet knew that British cloth, and British style, enjoy a unique reputation overseas. She felt sure there was a place in the market for their designs.

The name Dash & Miller arose from a search for a name that would represent what the duo were setting out to achieve, but that was not difficult to spell or pronounce for the target international audience. 'Dash' is a reference to haberdashery, and 'miller' to the mills where British cloth is woven. 'The name felt right,' says Juliet. 'It seemed to work, it was easy to spell and there's a sound of heritage to it, I think, but it's also slightly modern.'

There are now two parts to the business: the original design studio (Dash & Miller), and the Bristol Weaving Mill, where short runs of bespoke fabric are produced. Of the studio, Juliet says, 'We use hand looms as our primary tool for designing woven textiles. But we also do lots of other things: we create digital textiles, we do printing, embroidery and other mixed processes, like bonding. Our primary activity is the research and creation of innovative designs. We actively research materials, the wider industry, the world context, and new developments in all areas, but specifically design and materials innovations. These can relate to new technologies in any industry, like automotive or aviation, where there are new material developments and yarns. So we often work with yarn companies or emerging businesses who are developing new fibres, new systems. We look at wider trends and anything that might influence the world of design. We pull it all together and amalgamate it into our woven design collection.'

Juliet Bailey of Dash & Miller gives a weaving demonstration to the Lord Mayor of London, Alastair King, at the Woolmen's annual Sheep Drive and Livery Fair, September 2025.

'Adore', an exhibition by Garry Fabian Miller at the Arnolfini Gallery, Bristol (2023). The fabrics were woven by Dash & Miller.

The staff are all designer-weavers who spend much of their time travelling – New York, Milan, Paris, Amsterdam, Frankfurt, London – visiting clients or showing their designs at trade fairs such as Heimtextil, Première Vision and Milano Unica. Designs are sold outright, with full reproduction rights. 'Customers can do what they please with them, which is really useful for a lot of businesses, from Chanel to Marks & Spencer. Lots of design companies have budgets for that sort of thing, because they don't have the capability to generate what they need in-house. It helps them to diversify and bring in outside influences.' These purchases often lead to project work. 'They will commission us to put their factory set-up on our looms and then we can weave specifically into their set-ups with their specifications, so that it's a lot easier to make the jump from handloom to industrial.'

Another important activity is research and development, focused on sustainability in textiles. This includes testing recycled fibres, developing supply chains and using blockchain technology to make product origins traceable.

The Bristol Weaving Mill grew out of Dash & Miller. Two impulses lay behind it. 'When we initially approached larger mills to get our ideas developed, we found it could be difficult and expensive. We also came up against a certain reluctance to sample something new and innovative. We felt that it was something we could do, and we actually wanted to do. So we started our own mill. That allowed us to do the development phase and have more control over sampling lead times, fibres and so on. And then hand off a nicely resolved order to somebody who's expert at manufacturing....' They also found clients asking the company to replicate their designs exactly as they were: 'We would make a tweed for a couture designer, and quite often they would ask us, could we oversee the production?'

Making their own cloth allowed the company to diversify. It also introduced them to the Slow Textile Movement and Fibershed:[69] working with farmers who are committed to regenerative practices, using wool, alpaca, linen and other natural fibres, favouring local suppliers 'so that we can control the whole process, from the fibre on the farm all the way through to the finished product'. Deeply engaged in environmental issues, they also test experimental yarns from plant sources such as potatoes, hemp and nettles.

Visiting the company in Bristol I was surprised to discover that the Bristol Weaving Mill is in a building no bigger than a two-bedroom house. It contains a Dornier industrial loom, a collection of yarns, samples and tools. It is, says Juliet, 'really a small sampling and prototyping facility. We have no aspirations to run fifty weaving looms.'[70] When they need bulk production, they work with industrial mills and commission weavers in the UK.

Most of The Bristol Weaving Mill's production goes into blankets, cushions, upholstery fabric and fashion accessories such as scarves – occasionally a tailoring fabric. 'Our real strength at the mill is interior products, that's really something we can bring a lot of value to.'

Although there is a distinctive style in the Dash & Miller designs – a subtle, elegant and somehow 'just right' blend of classic and contemporary yarns, weaves and textures– their designers also pride themselves on being able to enter the house style of a client and create fabrics that fit the collection and extend its range. They have worked with Chanel, Hugo Boss, Thom Browne, Tommy Hilfiger, Vivienne Westwood, Joseph and other major fashion brands. It's all done very quietly, modestly and plainly, with a calm confidence in the quality and beauty of their designs.

I ask if there are any limits to what they can or will do. Would they accept a commission to design something that they would regard as being in bad taste, for example? The answer is surprising. 'We would weave any pattern and design regardless of whether it was aligned to our personal taste. But there are a couple of things that we do: the first is to make a bit of an assessment about the customer and their background, their knowledge. If a startup without much business experience or knowledge of textiles asks us to do something, we may feel it's our obligation to ask: "Are you sure you want to do that? Do you know what the outcomes are going to be?" We make sure that we are being responsible, and not just manufacturing it when we can see perhaps it won't land with the market. But then the other side of that is that at D&M we have a bad taste rule: if you feel that way, grab the most bad taste yarn you can find and find the thing that clashes with it the most and just weave that. You can almost guarantee that bad taste sample will sell – because people want something that they've not seen before.'

It is never easy to gauge how much of a success story is due to luck and how much is due to talent, training and hard work. There are skills in timing, knowing a good option from a bad one, finding the right people to work with and inspiring them to give their best. Juliet and Franki have had their share of luck, but there is an air of competence, openness, enthusiasm and commitment in all they do that almost certainly brings its own good luck with it.

A grant from the Queen Elizabeth Scholarship Trust (QEST) in 2013 allowed them to make a research trip around the British Isles, investigating every aspect of the textile industry: fibre extraction, spinning, dyeing, weaving and finishing. They built up a precious store of contacts and suppliers. In 2024 Dash & Miller entered a partnership with the silk weavers Sudbury Silk Mills – an intriguing marriage of heritage and innovation, with each bringing its own special capabilities to the union. 'They're guiding us through the next growth phase,' says Juliet. 'We're still effectively operating exactly as we were, but they're helping us with strategy, health and safety, training, back office, IT, HR... They are incredibly experienced and they've got this wonderful culture, which I think we have here too, but theirs stretches through the operations, where they have these systems in place, so it almost happens like clockwork... For them we can do a lot of innovative development such as exploring new techniques, yarns, warps, even samples for customers. Testing a warp yarn or new quality, for example, is a huge operation for them, and costly, whereas we can weave a sample in a day or two on our handlooms.'

Margo Selby

'Art into industry'. These three words are chosen to describe her life's work by Margo Selby, a designer weaver whose designs include spectacular hangings in Blackburn and Canterbury Cathedrals, handwoven artworks for collectors, cushions, rugs, blankets, scarves and even household linens sold in supermarkets and department stores. The range is extraordinary, as are the dazzling combinations of colour.

Number 114, Joseph Wilson Industrial Estate, Whitstable is a prefabricated metal building in a row of warehouses and car repair shops recently erected on the edge of town. It's not the sort of place where you would expect to find an art or design studio. Inside, however, it's a different story: a light and lofty space where the eye is mesmerised by the fabrics on display, the ear intrigued by the calm and regular clicking and thudding of a wooden loom. Margo Selby is the owner and founder of this studio, which reflects her belief in the craft of weaving and the uplifting effects of colour. She employs six young graduate weavers who work in all departments – photography,

Margo Selby. Portrait by Mark Cocksedge (2025).

marketing, sales, design, administration – taking turns to weave on the handloom. The building, both workshop and retail outlet, is open to visitors Monday to Friday, and is used periodically for exhibitions and weaving courses.

Margo Selby grew up in London in the 1980s. Her love of textiles was nurtured by her grandfather, a tailor on Savile Row, and her grandmother, who had a family collection of embroidery and lace and taught her to knit and crochet. At Chelsea College of Art she threw herself into the foundation year activities – drawing, fine art, printing, sculpture– but the moment she first used a loom, she says, 'I knew immediately that I loved it more than anything else. I really liked the mathematical, technical side of it, the problem-solving, the boundaries of the loom, the horizontal and vertical lines, the binary element of it.... That is something I have always loved to push and explore to see what I can do.'[71]

In 1999 she embarked on a master's degree at the Royal College of Art, learning how to operate industrial and Jacquard looms from the technician, Roger Lewis, whose expert knowledge and encouragement led to many a successful career. The RCA was, she recalls, an inspiring place, full of highly talented people working hard in a variety of artistic disciplines. Through the RCA she met Harriet Wallace-Jones and Emma Sewell, who offered her an internship. She also received help from the Crafts Council and from the Ann Sutton Foundation, which offered studio space to young graduates. She began designing furnishing fabrics for E & S Smith Ltd in Yorkshire and for a mill in India, and was commissioned to produce tablecloths for the National Portrait Gallery. Despite these opportunities, she says, '[I]t was hard finding my way, and hard to make a living.'

Gradually things improved. A significant milestone was partnering with Osborne & Little, the London wallpaper and fabric specialist. 'They introduced me to the best mills in the world, all different qualities. They knew where the best velvet weavers were, where the most creative colourful weavers were, and their international distribution is really seamless, with reps and showrooms in every place in the world that's interested in fabric.' Another milestone was when she started to make large artworks. The first of these was the 'Vexillum' series (*vexillum* is Latin for a military standard or banner; she thinks of them as 'celebratory flags'). 'I started on these in 2015. I was weaving some upholstery designs and I decided I was getting annoyed with the boundaries that you have when designing for a commercial product – you have to think about how durable it is, or how it will repeat, or whether the factory can handle that number of colours. I decided to let go of all those boundaries and just make a beautiful piece of fabric for its own sake and see where that led me… The more authentic you are, the more you let go of all the boundaries, the more interesting the ideas are. They will then feed into commercial products in a new and fresh way.'

She also finds fulfilment in collaborations, most recently in the giant 'Moon Landing' banner (14.3 metres long) designed to hang in the centre of the spiral staircase at Somerset House for the Collect Art Fair in 2024. This was devised in dialogue with a piece of music by the composer Helen Caddick, a sextet for strings. Both artists were inspired by the 1969 Apollo XI mission to the moon and the part played in its success by Navajo women 'who used their weaving skills and ability to visualise complicated patterns to create the integrated circuit designs used in the guidance and control systems of the Apollo spacecraft.' This exhilarating work was moved to Canterbury Cathedral in 2025 to be suspended from the ceiling above the Archbishop's throne.[72]

Moon Landing installation at Canterbury Cathedral (June 2025) by Margo Selby and Helen Caddick. *Moon Landing* is woven on a cotton warp with a weft of British wool. The wool was supplied by Shepley Yarns, a company whose palette Margo Selby describes as 'an incredible rich and bright array of colour'. Her words apply equally well to the finished piece.

Hand-knotted rugs made of wool and silk in India to Margo Selby's designs.

Like many a creative weaver, Margo Selby is fascinated by the traditional textiles of India. She commissions hand-made carpets from Indian weavers, inspired by their exquisite craftsmanship and intense colours, and by a desire to preserve their skills. 'Most of the work we do in India you couldn't do in the UK,' she says. 'They have special hand-weaving techniques in making rugs that we just don't have.' It's not, she stresses, a question of price: Indian weavers aren't always cheaper or better. 'We buy velvet from Belgium, for example, because they do it best. For me it's about the craft skills these different places offer.'[73]

Dashing Tweeds

The neighbourhood of London's Marylebone High Street is an enclave of bohemian-chic reminiscent of Chelsea in the 1960s. Prices are high, but so is the quality, and style outranks all else. Here you can find a specialist in Japanese gardening tools, a retro hardware and kitchen shop, designer clothing boutiques, and cafés offering curated espresso and croissants that would pass muster in Paris or Milan. At 47 Dorset Street is Dashing Tweeds, where Guy Hills and Kirsty McDougall have created a zany but remarkably successful business, designing and selling 'urban tweeds'. Their aesthetic

These special edition sneakers by Converse gave Dashing Tweeds their first commercial success. The pattern is Regent's Park Check, a playful take on the classic Glen Urquhart plaid made famous in the 1890s by the Prince of Wales (later King Edward VII).

is rooted in the colours and weave patterns of traditional Scottish tweeds, but shot through with a glittering cocktail of influences from punk, rave, electronics, bio-luminescence, Formula 1, the history of European painting and the fabrics of the Middle and Far East – to name just a few. Their ideas first caught the public eye in 2011, when Converse, the fashionable American maker of street-style shoes, commissioned a tweed sneaker. Thirty thousand pairs of these gave the company a flying start. 'I stockpiled as many as possible,' says Guy Hills, 'and sold them to my very impressed friends. The following year I opened the first Dashing Tweeds shop in Sackville Street.' Since then they have dressed characters in films such as *Mary Poppins, Paddington,* and *The Boat That Rocked,* designed a Goodwood Revival outfit for the racing driver Jacques Villeneuve, and done much to restore to English life the brilliance and colour of eighteenth-century tailoring.

Guy Hills knew what he wanted to achieve: 'to bring a greater choice of textiles into gentlemen's lives – more colour, more texture, more vibrancy – and to modernise tweed'. His aesthetic education began in childhood as his grandmother escorted him around the museums of Europe. He inherited a tweed jacket from his father, which he wore throughout his studies in biology at the University of Bristol. After graduation he turned away from science to pursue a passion for photography. He served an apprenticeship with the Association of Photographers, and after years of studio work as an assistant, began specialising in shoots for Savile Row tailors. Occasionally he persuaded a client to pay him with a suit rather than cash.

'Tailors have incredible skill,' he says. 'They have *gravitas*, they have validity, they turn your dreams into reality, but fifteen years ago the fabrics they offered were dull. I was looking for exciting outfits. Ladies were allowed to have them, but not men. There is no good reason for this: just look at the history of Savile Row. When it started two hundred years ago the tailors offered a wonderful variety of colours: scarlet, bright blue, emerald green, yellow... I thought we could do that.'[74] At the Royal College of Art degree show in 2002 he was impressed by the work of Kirsty McDougall – particularly a fridge with a colourfully upholstered interior – and asked her if she could design him a really stunning piece of suiting cloth. She loved the idea, and recommended yarns and a mill in Yorkshire that would weave it. But the mill would not weave less than sixty metres. He wanted six for a suit.... so why not sell the remaining fifty-four? 'It was all a bit of a joke, with Kirsty saying things like "We're on the crest of a weave" in her fabulous Hebridean accent. Then we sold a few bolts of cloth and it gradually became a proper business.'

The modern 'urban
tweed' in action, woven
with luminous threads
for visibility in the dark.

The Tweed Run, a fancy dress bicycle race, *concours d'élégance* and picnic. Held annually in London since 2009, it has been enthusiastically replicated in locations around the world, including New York, Tokyo, Tuscany and the island of Spetses in Greece. Suggested attire for the Tweed Run from the organisers, Bourne & Hollingsworth: 'woollen plus fours, Harris Tweed jackets, Fair Isle jumpers, alpaca coats, merino wool team jerseys; cycling skirts and perhaps a sporty cycling cape for the ladies, cravats or ties for gentlemen, and a sneaky hip flask of sustenance for afterwards.'

Guy is a passionate cyclist, and likes to ride in tweeds. London is a hazardous place on two wheels, however, and he was not keen on synthetic high-visibility vests; so he thought of making a reflecting tweed jacket. Although this proved a technical challenge, the difficulties were overcome and he christened the result 'Lumatwill'– a stylish and strikingly visible fabric that has sold well.

Tweeds are traditionally regarded as country wear, but as Guy and his friends were happy to demonstrate, they look just as good in the city. 'So we came up with the idea of urban tweeds for the gentleman about town. This was a crystallisation of all our thinking. We had hundreds of ideas whizzing around but we had to boil them down so that people could understand what we were doing. You have to do that if you want actually to sell anything.' This 'crystallisation' became even more necessary when he decided to open a shop. 'That was rather foolhardy. I had no idea how much you have to sell just to pay the rent. I was good at getting press, though, so people would read about us and that brought customers in...'

A showman and aesthete, he serves tea and cherry tart on bone china while flashing through his vast portfolio of photographs: the Tweed Run (a vintage London bicycle race – the riders in Edwardian outfits), the Chap Olympiad,[75] a male model striding through the London Underground in a loud purple and blue check suit, himself on skis in the Swiss Alps, wearing a Norfolk jacket and plus fours in lime green and salmon pink herringbone tweed... 'Wool is most practical for skiing– warm, waterproof, breathable. People are brainwashed into wearing plastics. For some reason they wear what everyone else wears without questioning it.' Creativity seems to flow easily and happily from him – with no limits. A former raver, he goes to Glastonbury festival every year and has a family rock band just to mop up any spare energy.

Other members of the London team are Holly Pressdee (business manager) and Naomi Greenland (production and design), both weavers and graduates in textile design. Although Guy and his team front the business, Kirsty McDougall, based in Hastings, provides a creative engine for the seasonal collections, transforming the group's design ideas into woven samples. Robbie Trussler, of Drove Weaving in the Scottish Borders, completes the process by putting the designs into production. Guy Hills describes him as 'incredibly supportive, always happy to have a go. He creates beautiful lasting fabrics. Without him there would be no Dashing Tweeds.'[76]

'Intersectional Family' by the Glaswegian/Nigerian artist Olubiyi Thomas, a set of figures in copper masks and tartan robes walking on air towards the viewer at the V&A's 2024 'Tartan' exhibition in Dundee. The robes were woven by Kirsty McDougall. The exhibition curator comments, 'The Intersectional Family are dressed in green and white tartan, a colour scheme shared by the Nigerian flag and Glasgow's Celtic football club, reflecting Thomas' cross-cultural identity. The tartan's weave and the use of recycled fabric also symbolises the deconstructing and reconstructing of different histories and identities.'

Kirsty McDougall was born on the Isle of Lewis and took a master's degree in 2002 at the Royal College of Art, where she later taught and headed the Weave department. Although she enjoyed academic work, she became frustrated by the 'constant squeeze of too many students and not enough time', and established her own design studio in East London, providing research and development to the textile industry, weaving samples and selling designs to architects, artists, interior designers and couturiers. Her list of clients includes Fendi, Givenchy, Marc Jacobs, Vivienne Westwood, Balmain, Balenciaga, Louis Vuitton and numerous design agencies. She moved to Hastings during the pandemic of 2020–1, renting an entire floor of a former Victorian warehouse. 'Hastings is a place of possibility and germination,' she says. 'There's a big textile community and a great Do It Yourself attitude.'[77]

Like many other weavers, Kirsty loves the precision and discipline of her craft – she calls it a form of 'soft engineering' – and has a highly developed sense of community and shared existence, not just with colleagues in the trade, but with the natural world, which is the source of both raw materials and inspiration. Irked by too much talk about sustainability– 'there's so much greenwashing going on!' – she is nevertheless deeply committed to the cause, using waste, recycled and natural yarns wherever possible while also indulging her fascination for the extraordinary effects that can be achieved with synthetics.

Conclusion

What do these designer weavers have in common? Certain characteristics stand out: a fascination with colour, and a determination to bring more of it into people's lives; a commitment to quality of design and materials, to durable fabrics made with sustainability in mind; and a third element, surprisingly effective in a competitive world – they have all managed to retain a fresh, exploratory, playful approach, which shines through everything they produce. Talking to their customers and supporters, as well as to the designer-weavers themselves, it is clear that this is the quality, sensed in the liveliness and beauty of the colours, that communicates so powerfully and unlocks such energy and enthusiasm in the soul.

CHAPTER 6

Studying Textile Design: (1) Style

In 1830s Britain, as the textile industry underwent rapid mechanisation, the government was alarmed to note that British manufacturers were taking a declining share in the global textile trade. The advantage gained while France pursued its revolution and Napoleon rampaged across Europe had somehow been lost, leaving observers to question the benefits of industrialisation. The analysis was that while the technical skills of British weavers were unparalleled, their design capabilities were lacking. An article in the *Illustrated London News* from 1843 put it clearly: 'The textile fabrics of our manufacturing industry are superior, in the strength and beauty of their structure, to those of all nations, whether of ancient or modern date; but in their forms and decorations they are deficient in taste, and are this moment surpassed by many of the smaller states of Europe. Saxony is superior to us in harmony of colour, Germany in ornamental combinations, and France in the variety, grace, and fitness of its embellishments... This national inferiority has arisen from our neglect of nature in the education of our ornamental designers, and from a mercenary habit of leaving the invention of our patterns to the accidental, unpaid, and uncultivated imaginations of the poor foremen of factories.'[78] The solution proposed was a massive investment in design education.

Britain's major art and design schools were founded at this time. The Government School of Design was established in London in 1837, under the superintendence of the Board of Trade, to serve all the major manufacturing sectors of the nation. Similar institutions were set up around the country – at Manchester in 1838, Birmingham and Nottingham in 1843, Glasgow in 1845, Leeds in 1846 and so on. At the 1851 Great Exhibition, Nottingham impressed the jurors with the quality of its textile designs. The Government School of Design was judged to have 'materially assisted the enterprising manufacturer and artisan'.[79] With the profits from the Great Exhibition, the South Kensington Museum was

SCHOOL OF DESIGN.

The Government School of Design in Somerset House, the Strand, London. Following the Great Exhibition of 1851, this initially small-scale operation greatly expanded its remit to accommodate art as well as design. After a series of name changes and shifts in focus, the institution was renamed the Royal College of Art in 1896.

established to provide examples of the best craftsmanship and design from around the world, absorbing the Government School of Design in 1853. Meanwhile the other art schools grew rapidly, with student numbers across Britain rising from 3,296 in 1851 to 31,455 by 1855.[80]

Despite the ambition to marry art and industry, however, the roles of technician and designer remained distinct – both in education and manufacture. The workers in the textile mills were ill-paid factory hands, assigned to narrow tasks in a mechanised production line, who learned on the job. Designers learned through art college. While Mechanics' Institutes and other centres of self-improvement strove to bridge the gap, tensions remained. Manufacturers complained that design students were not sufficiently equipped with commercial insight, while designers felt that their efforts to improve taste fell on deaf ears. Manufacturers, moreover, resented being asked to help fund courses that they feared encouraged people to become artists, lost to landscape painting rather than profitably employed in industry.[81] As a Parliamentary Select Committee Report had suggested in 1836, 'Unless the Arts and Manufactures be practically combined, the unsuccessful aspirants after the higher branches of the Arts will be infinitely multiplied, and the deficiency of manufacturing-articles will not be supplied.'[82]

Since those days, art and design schools have been reformed many times, in efforts to combine arts and manufacturing in practical ways. When the architectural historian Nikolaus Pevsner investigated the role of the designer in the industrial process in Britain in the 1930s, one of his central tasks was to 'verify the extent to which [art schools] were co-operating with industry.'[83] He noted that at that time, in the United Kingdom, 'woven fabrics of the highest artistic standards, standards not surpassed anywhere, are not at all rare'.[84] So they must have been doing something right. At the same time, he regretted that the schools on the whole lacked the equipment and skilled teachers necessary to train designers for industrial as opposed to hand-craft production – an observation that no one would be likely to make today.

Despite technological advances, however, belief in the value of the handloom as a tool for learning, championed by the Arts and Crafts movement in the late nineteenth century and the Bauhaus in the twentieth, has been constant. The pioneering artist-weaver Ethel Mairet was convinced that learning the techniques of handloom weaving was beneficial to practitioners across the industrial/craft spectrum. She stressed this in her influential book *Hand-Weaving To-day* (London, 1939). She was the first woman to be awarded the title Royal Designer for Industry

Ethel Mairet spinning at Gospels Workshop in Ditchling, Sussex. Influential as much for her 1916 book *A Book on Vegetable Dyes* as for her later book on hand-weaving, during the 1930s and 1940s Mairet trained people in both weaving and dyeing at her Ditchling workshop.

by the Royal Society of Arts in 1938. Later, figures such as Mary Barker and Marianne Straub, who studied hand-weaving with Mairet, came to play significant roles in industrial textile design. Straub, who wrote that she wanted 'to design things that people could afford' and that 'to remain a handweaver did not seem satisfactory in this age of mass-production', produced textiles for both the London Underground and British European Airways.[85]

Out of these cross-currents of debate have arisen the array of courses in textile design available today; in 2025, the Universities and Colleges Admissions Service (UCAS) listed 280 courses from eighty-five providers. While a few (mainly postgraduate) courses focus on the purely technical side of the textile industry, most favour a broad design education within fashion and design departments, with technical elements such as dyeing and strength testing given a greater or lesser emphasis. What these share with the pioneering courses of the mid-Victorian period is the ambition to improve the standards, and therefore the commercial value, of textile production in the United Kingdom.

The Benzie Building, Manchester School of Art, home to Manchester Metropolitan University's textile department.

Manchester Metropolitan University

Manchester School of Art was set up in 1838 to provide design training for the city's cotton manufacturing industry, fourteen years after the establishment of the Manchester Mechanics' Institute, which was a school of science. While Manchester itself was primarily a spinning town, it served mills producing cloth in the towns all around, with a strong need for designers. Today the School of Art is part of Manchester Metropolitan University. The textile department inhabits a suite of light-filled rooms in the glass-walled Benzie Building, a RIBA award-winning building opened in 2013 to celebrate the School of Art's 175th birthday.

Manchester's 'Textiles in Practice' course was born in 2014 from the amalgamation of three previous courses – Textile Design, Embroidery, and Textiles for Fashion. Lecturer Sophia Fenlon explains: 'We wanted to benefit our students by playing on the crossover between courses – introducing them to the whole palette of machinery, equipment and space they can access.' There is an insistence on technical skills, with workshop inductions delivered increasingly by technicians.

This emphasis has been driven by the students. Since the rise in student fees in 2012–13, graduate outcomes and industry-friendly skill sets have become critical. In addition, ten years ago 90 per cent of students would have done a foundation course between school and university; now it's more like 60 per cent. This means that many students have not had an opportunity to explore multiple art and design technologies, or to focus on drawing, the bedrock of all art and design. Many also lack technical skills and an appreciation of the specific demands and career potential of textiles. Fenlon notes that while she was able to do a textile design technology course at 'A' level, increasingly these more technical courses have been cut. Furthermore, it was while she was on her foundation year at Manchester that she switched from a primary interest in fashion to textiles: 'I discovered what textiles really were,' she says. Her course is designed to make up for these lost opportunities to experiment and discover.

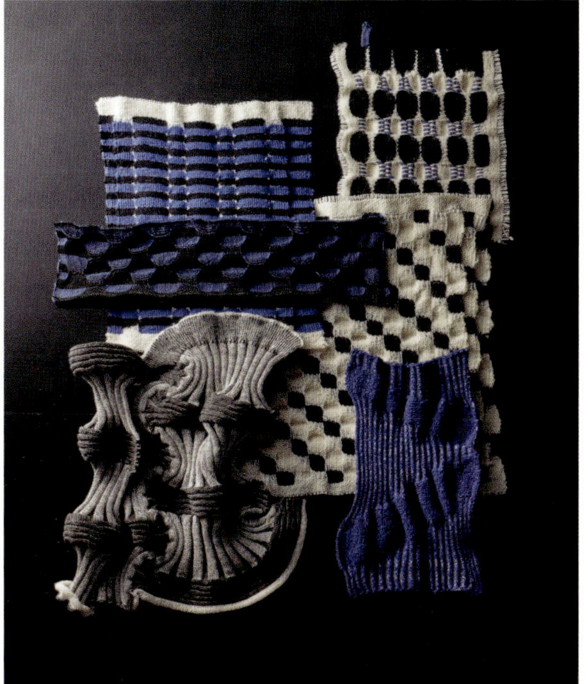

Tactile Constructs: Work by Lily Everard, 2025 BA Textiles in Practice, mixing woven and knitted textiles. Winner of the Design Breakthrough Award at Manchester Metropolitan University. In her written statement she says, 'I am particularly interested in the engineered side of textiles– how they adapt, and how structure and material choice influence performance and user experience. I see my future in a role that allows me to further explore these qualities, ideally within industries where textiles serve a vital technical role.'

Despite this, student numbers seem to be in long-term decline. Fenlon argues that this is owing to misconceptions about the workplace value of textile design courses, commenting, 'Students who do engineering could come to us – the best weaving students have often done science or maths alongside art subjects at "A" Level – but engineering is rated higher than design, and design higher than textiles. We need to encourage students to see the utility for them of a design and textiles education.'

To help non-foundation students to catch up their foundation year peers, the course offers fewer but more in-depth modules. In their first term, students are introduced to all the textile workshops: weave, knit, embroidery, print and mixed-media. Here they begin to explore the translation of drawing and colour into a collection of material samples. In the second term, students begin to look at how they would use a specific workshop to answer a brief, and to identify how their use of workshops would be influenced by their research and drawings: the leap from conceptualisation to construction. Students are also required to take a course on the methods and strategies of sustainable textile practices and 'how they embed sustainability in their practice'. This topic runs as a thread through all years of all courses within the Design Department, strengthened by recently appointed staff such as Paul Micklethwaite, who has written extensively on recycling and sustainability in fashion and textiles.

Future X is a distinctive feature of the Manchester course. From their first year, textile students have the opportunity to work in an interdisciplinary way with other students across Manchester School of Art, collaborating with an outside business on a project. In 2024 this unit was devised with Hallmark greetings cards. The students together created ten objects in different media: from textiles to artefacts to animation. 'It is about narrative and communication. It is about introducing them to the idea that their work needs to be understood by a wider audience,' Fenlon explains.

Seven or eight students, out of a year group of thirty to forty-five, tend to choose weaving as their specialism at the end of their first year. The teachers and technicians ensure weaving students have a strong skill set before they begin to incorporate other textile techniques, such as knit or embroidery.

There are twelve table looms available for first year students. A second room is available for second- and third-year undergraduates and MA students, with ARM Touch 60 looms, older dobby looms, eight portable table looms, one wide dobby loom and a Jacquard. This array allows students to experiment with technologies from different centuries. In 2024 two students volunteered with Historic England to restore two nineteenth-century Jacquard silk handlooms at Paradise Mill in

Above: Bea Uprichard and Ruth Farris working on one of the heritage Jacquard looms at the Silk Museum in Macclesfield. Since graduating in 2024 they have set up their own company, Fishbone and Sycamore, creating woven silk textiles on the David Jones loom there. Silk weaving, once an important industry throughout Cheshire, is now an endangered craft on the Heritage Crafts Red List.

Above right: Niall Trowsdale Stannard modelling for his final degree show in 2024. He says of his neon tweeds and other weaves, 'Project Alien explores the journey of expressing and celebrating your own identity. Here, my identity as a gay drag artist is a physical representation of the alienation of queer people.' Trowsdale Stannard was a recipient of a bursary award from the Weavers' Company that enabled him to gain hands-on experience of modern technology.

Right: New Designers 2025: textiles by Martha Lawton, of Manchester Metropolitan University, who won the Camira Circular Design Prize for her final project, 'At the River', a series of woven artworks on the theme of waterway pollution. The prize celebrates innovation in responsible textile design: 'Martha's work hits every mark, blending sustainability with creativity in powerful and personal ways.'

Macclesfield, where seventy-one silk mills and 5,000 looms once operated. Others take advantage of the high-tech capabilities of more modern machines to design complex digital weaves.

Students are taught to record every facet of the journey from creative research to the final outcome – workings-out on paper, warp plans, swatches – in order to have a full understanding of the entire process of creating a cloth. Many third years will spend up to a week in the dyeing room, for instance. This emphasis on technical skill is reflected in the new status of technicians, who are being granted membership of the Higher Education Academy. This professional recognition enables them to apply for Fellowships and undertake technical research.

Some students become teachers, usually after further degrees. Others go into a variety of jobs, from fashion design to self-employed handloom weaving. Through an Entry to Work Scheme organised and financed by the Weavers' and Clothworkers' Companies, the course now has good links with commercial textile mills. A recent graduate, Polly Almond, took advantage of this scheme to join A.W. Hainsworth, while Alex Daniels works as an account manager at Humphries Weaving in Suffolk. Many graduates go on to work in textiles for interiors or in colour consultancy. Whichever direction they choose, Fenlon hopes that all are equipped to be independent in their practice. 'Though well-qualified to be weavers,' she says, 'they will never just be seen as weavers. They are designers too.'

Nottingham Trent University

In the early modern period, Nottingham throve as a centre of hosiery, knitting and lace. In 1589 William Lee, a curate from Calverton, a village just outside Nottingham, invented the stocking frame, the basis for all subsequent knitting machines. Later, in the eighteenth century, as men chose increasingly to wear trousers and hosiery manufacture went into decline, Nottingham's lace industry expanded. By the late nineteenth century, Nottingham's Lace Market was the centre of the global lace industry. This historic legacy has contributed to the contemporary strength of Nottingham Trent's textile department. The day we visit, the Wall Street Journal is in, filming the antique lace looms and examining the archive. The university has its origins in the Government School of Design opened in the city in 1843. As Tina Downes, deputy head of fashion, textiles and knitwear design, remarks, 'We have been teaching art for industry for a long time.'

NTU Weave Room with then third year student, Elin Griffiths, in 2024.

The current course in textile design was developed in the 1970s. It combines the practical skills of weave, knit, print and embroidery with a thorough grounding in general design principles. The department is equipped with an impressive array of equipment: sixteen lightweight handlooms, thirteen ARM Touch 60 hand looms, an industrial-level Jacquard, four digital TC2 Jacquard handlooms and several old-school dobby looms donated to the college in 1968.

As at Manchester, fewer than a third of students have done foundation courses (it was two-thirds in the past). While most students coming from 'A' level show evidence of basic skill in computer-aided design, stitch, print and knit, it is very rare for them to have used a loom. During the pandemic of 2020–1, with students stuck in their rooms or at home, the department invested in home-weaving kits for students and recorded instructions for setting up a loom. The entire 2020–1 intake ended that year knowing how to weave, print and knit.

Fabrics by Meg James, who graduated in Textile Design from Nottingham Trent University in 2024. Originally from Cornwall and inspired by the life and colours of the sea, she now works in London for Watts 1874, who create and sell historically inspired luxury wallpapers, decorative fabrics, trimmings and tapestries.

Studies and fabrics by Evie Hensser, final year student at Nottingham Trent University. Hensser was the winner of the ROMO Award for Innovation in Design and Colour at New Designers, 2025.

These resources have proven valuable in other ways. The emergency action has contributed to current research in the department into pedagogy for neurodiverse students – 'Our motto is success for all' – an important development when many such students find their progress through higher education hampered by traditional approaches.

The first year at Nottingham Trent offers two courses that run in parallel. The first, taught in groups drawn from across the departments of fashion, textiles and knitwear, focuses on core design components such as concept, drawing, materials, colour and future thinking. The students are encouraged to develop their own design identity. As the official course description words it: 'begin to see the future

THE WEAVER'S TRADE

as something you can shape, rather than something that just happens'. The second course, Creative Development and Application for Textile Design, allows students to participate in a series of workshops in print, weave, knit, embroidery and multimedia. Towards the end of the year they choose their pathway, involving more rigorous practical study. The second year allows further rotation to enable students to consolidate their skills and confirm their choice as well as offering access to master classes in other disciplines.

Nottingham Trent places great emphasis on the real-world contexts of textile practice. In the second year students participate in multi-disciplinary teams in a live project with industry partners: fashion retailer Next, for instance, or paint specialists Dulux. Students develop knowledge of emerging cultural issues such as responsible design practice, or international markets and trends,

and are introduced to the demands of professional communication. Their own creative development is furthered in a second module where they draw up research proposals that reflect personal design interests, and are encouraged to experiment within their chosen textile area.

In 2024 students were also offered the Co-Lab unit, which further develops risk-taking, as student teams were challenged with a brief related to themes of sustainability, social justice, enterprise and innovation or community. A further optional module allows students to explore their discipline from a range of professional and creative perspectives – from slow making and craftsmanship to creative entrepreneurship; from emerging textile technologies to issues surrounding longevity and circularity.

At the end of the second year, students can opt to have a placement in industry or proceed directly to the final year. This final year involves a research element and the production of a major body of work. Ideas such as biophilia (our closeness to nature), degrowth (a resistance to the idea that growth in GDP is the best measure of human progress) and the connection between design and well-being are among recent themes selected by students for their dissertations. There are also opportunities to enhance career prospects by taking part in live business projects, meeting professional bodies, exhibiting at New Designers in London and entering competitions. In 2024, final year students worked with Sainsbury's supermarkets, Paul Vogel design studio and clothes retailer Next.

Work of Ines Congratel, who graduated from Nottingham Trent University in 2025. She says of her years of study: 'Industry experience with Liberty, Casamance, and Romo has taught me to balance creativity with market viability. Recognitions such as the Weavers' Company Scholarship Award for Excellence, showcasing my work in Paris alongside Paul Vogel, and being a finalist in an AI-driven project have fuelled my passion for textile design and amplified my ambition to work in the industry.' At New Designers 2025 she won the Sanderson Award, which includes a twelve-month paid internship with the interiors business Sanderson. The criteria for the prize are: 'We are looking for a collection that recognises the aspirations and requirements of today's customer and demonstrates creativity, innovation and commercial understanding through a strong concept, exceptional use of colour, and iconic designs that are inspiring and new.'

A detail from Ines Congratel's work.

'We have to give them flexible, adaptable skills,' says Angharad McLaren, senior lecturer in textile design. 'This is an education not a training.' At the same time, McLaren says, 'We know we have industry-ready students.' She suggests that the post-2020 course, with its collaborative elements and encouragement to students to develop their own learning, has enabled graduates to make immediate and valuable contributions in their workplaces, whether in trend forecasting, 3D materials or sustainability.

One of the difficulties all textile courses face is attracting prospective students. As fashion applications rise, textile applications are 'going down and down', says McLaren. In addition, 99 per cent of the applications are from women, despite attempts to attract men by boosting the technical aspects of the course. All textile departments would prefer more of a gender balance. McLaren describes the challenge: 'Woven materials are everywhere, but they are invisible. We now go into local schools to teach teachers what the possibilities are.'[86]

McLaren details the careers of some recent graduates. Jenny Banks (2015) is currently a research engineer at the National Composites Centre, following materials research roles at Finisterre and Fab Lab London. Hannah Hughes (2021) was another 'very technically-led student with a strong sustainability focus who loved to explore complex structures'. After a stint as a technician in Nottingham Trent's department, she became a weaving development technician at specialist narrow fabric webbing manufacturers M. Wright & Sons. Lucy Knights (2018), who produced a final collection focused on British heritage textiles, currently holds a position in business development and outside sales at textile design studio Perennials. Her first role after graduating was a production team assistant with British design studio Wallace Sewell, funded by the Entry to Work Scheme. She has also worked at Margo Selby and Bute Fabrics. The department's lead weave technician is Taylor Cowton, who won a Worshipful Company of Weavers' student scholarship and graduated from the course in 2019. She credits the university with enabling her to realise her vocation. 'I wasn't into decorating fabric. I wanted to make it,' she says.

The Glasgow School of Art

The Fashion and Textiles Department of Glasgow School of Art sits at the top of a new building on Renfrew Street, facing the famous Mackintosh Building (1899–1909).[87] History is an important presence here. As Dr Helena Britt, programme leader for textile design, has written: 'Textiles, their design, production and study have been closely connected to The Glasgow School of Art (GSA) since its formation as a branch of the Government School of Design in 1845.'[88] Many graduates have themselves gone on to teach, including Nottingham Trent University's Angharad McLaren, and several lecturers and technicians at GSA. Other graduates have gained employment in companies such as Johnstons of Elgin, Alex Begg, Holland & Sherry, Stephen Walters, Burberry, Bute Fabrics, Harris Tweed Hebrides, lululemon, and Robert Mackie.

The Textile Design BA, in common with many courses at Scottish universities, extends over four years, the first focusing on drawing, colour and research, all skills necessary for textile design. It is in the second year that students get to grips with the different textile disciplines, with two weeks on each of weave, print, knit, and embroidery. Students choose their specialism at the end of their second year, and are strongly encouraged to choose just one. Elaine Bremner, current textiles lecturer and subject leader in Weave, recognises that weave in particular offers challenges: 'Weave is quite a slow process, it requires patience and can take longer to get to grips with the basic technical skills, but after that it offers exciting possibilities.'[89] In 2024 she had just four final weavers. In 2025 she had eight.

As they reach the fourth year, students have gained the independence to set their own programme of study. Bremner observes that students coming to GSA from other countries, including Japan, often have a high degree of skill but are not used to building their own identity as textile designers. She says, 'Some start from a technical question, which is great. But how are you going to take this beyond a technical exercise? Where are the colours going to come from? How are they going to make it personal? That is where their research and drawing can take their work further.'

'I like it when students ask, *What if?*' she says, pointing out that because the second and third year grades do not count towards the final marks, students can take risks and try out things that

Textiles lecturer Elaine Bremner, subject leader in Weave at Glasgow School of Art.

Above: Work by Helena Powell, a final year student at Glasgow School of Art, displayed at New Designers 2024.

Left: A tutor inspecting some student trials at Glasgow School of Art.

may not work. 'We like to encourage ambition,' she adds, pointing to one student using metal chain through the weft.

Bremner is proud of the creative skills in drawing and research that the department cultivates. She also has the highest regard for the work of the technicians. 'They are around all the time,' she says, and their presence is crucial to the students. As well as managing the department's looms, demonstrating the safe use of machinery, materials and processes, and training students in CAD, they trouble-shoot and offer innovative solutions to design ideas.

Students at GSA are encouraged to think about their future careers and to take on live projects and collaborations with industry. One year Transcal, a company making car seats in Livingstone, set students the challenge of imagining what travel would look like in 2050. This required research but also production of a collection of fabrics. The winning student looked at luxury travel. She used natural fibres including hemp and boiled them all in sage, embedding the scents in the fabrics to promote well-being. Another gifted student, Anita Sarkezi, was commissioned in her fourth year to create a new banner for the Incorporation of Weavers of Glasgow (founded in 1514).

Originally from Slovenia, Sarkezi was awarded the School's Newbery Medal, given to an outstanding final year student, as well as the Clothworkers' Company first prize for a woven fabric design for interior furnishings.

Another high achiever has been Jonathan Mackinnon, who left a career in microbiology for textiles. In 2020 he embarked on the Master of Design programme at GSA and was commissioned by the Worshipful Company of Weavers to produce a work for the permanent collection of the V&A entitled *Waste Not, Want Not*. Accomplished during Covid in 2020–21, it involved gathering waste and deadstock from industrial mills, which he hand-wove at home with denim salvaged from friends and family on a hand-made frame loom. Awarded the Weavers' Company's most prestigious scholarship, the Stuart Hollander Award, he has set up his own design studio in Uddingston.

These last two examples illustrate the challenges for young weavers as they leave university. The equipment they need to pursue their vocation is often beyond their means. Mackinnon can experiment on a handloom, but Sarkezi's main interest is in the digital realm. Both have done work at Alex Begg & Co in Ayr, where many GSA graduates find opportunities and where Mackinnon is currently new product development manager. Others have taken up jobs at Bute Fabrics and Johnstons of Elgin. Sarkezi has more recently been appointed artist in residence at GSA where she can use the Jacquard loom in a free and creative way, as well as maintaining a studio design practice. Bremner sees the course as laying a foundation for all these different choices.

Jonny Mackinnon, a graduate of the Glasgow School of Art, with a selection of his fabrics woven from recycled materials.

Falmouth University

The context of Falmouth University's textile design course could not be more different. Set on a windy hill outside the old fishing port, far from any major city, the Penryn Campus is one reflection of the ambition and determination that has transformed the tiny private Falmouth School of Art, founded in 1902, into the fully fledged Falmouth University. Since its formal recognition in 2012, the university has chosen to focus on applied creativity and innovation, across disciplines including art, design, architecture, fashion, photography, performing arts, music, business, gaming and computing. Textile design is taught inside the purpose-built Fashion and Textiles Institute, which presents a curved glass front to the courtyard and reveals a cheerful open-plan space within.

Sally-Ann Gill has been in charge of the course since 2019. A graduate of University College for the Creative Arts at Farnham (now UCA Farnham) and the Royal College of Art, her energy and passion have secured financial support for the course, scholarships for students and wide recognition of her innovative, trans-disciplinary approach to teaching and curriculum design.

In 2022 she re-wrote the Textile Design syllabus. Her motives were three-fold. First, Gill reports that she 'wanted to embed sustainability and responsibility more explicitly into the modules'. (Gill notes that up to 80 per cent of students express ethical concerns in their applications.) Second, Gill had noticed that her students were perhaps more diverse both in their talents and in their ambitions than those

The Fashion and Textiles Institute at Falmouth University's Penryn Campus.

applying to other institutions – 'They end up doing all sorts of things' – and therefore that the traditional pathways model was of less service than a course delivering broader skills. Gill notes, 'The students need fundamental skills relating to all textile design.' Finally, Gill could see that owing to the narrowing options in schools and the rising costs of higher education, fewer students were applying to do textiles. To keep recruitment and retention strong, Gill needed to ensure she could produce employable students.

Instead, therefore, of plunging students into five-week rotations in different textile disciplines, the course opens with a module on colour and pattern. As well as studying colour theory and palettes, the students learn about dyeing – both chemical and natural. They are introduced to the natural dye garden that the department has created in the college grounds, with gardening on the timetable. A second module introduces the idea of responsible design and encourages the students to look at the provenance and life cycle of fibre. They learn to spin yarn on drop spindles and spinning wheels. This pre-industrial technology, dating back millennia, encourages them to become familiar with the substrate of all textile manufacture: thread. 'Some students really get into it,' Gill reports, 'and like to create their own yarns.' Sometimes the college receives donations of sheep or alpaca fleeces. Students can also spin flax. Nothing is wasted. The department even teaches papermaking as an extra so as not to waste scrap paper.

Students visit each workshop – weave, print and mixed media – three times. Each visit is for two weeks, so, in total, they try a discipline for six weeks, rather than one long five-week module, before they choose their specialism for the summer term. This is especially hard work for the weave technician, Wendy Kotenko, who has to prepare all the looms with different yarns so that students just encounter 'the fun bits'. (Kotenko is herself a graduate of Farnham, before doing her PGCHE at

Textile Design course leader, Sally-Ann Gill, in the dye garden at Falmouth University.

Falmouth, and has been here for nineteen years.) Gill has discovered that offering students these bit-sized introductory courses has actually balanced out the choices. Previously weave suffered because students tended to arrive with no experience of the discipline, whereas they had encountered print and embroidery. 'This way they approach it several times, from different angles.' In the 2024 third year group who had studied under the old course structure, six out of twenty-eight students were weavers. The second years, the first to experience the new course, fielded eleven weavers out of twenty-nine students.

The department owns twenty-one table looms, twelve floor looms, a TC2 Jacquard loom and a Bonas Dataweave Jacquard. Gill is passionate about hand skills. 'We believe that the artisan has a future. We believe that slow processes have a place in the future.' She is also determined, however, to equip her students with all the necessary computer-aided design skills to take their place in the industry. 'I have been tasked with coming up with a five-year plan to strengthen the course,'

Work of Ellie Rosa Pyner. Winner of a Commendation from the Weavers' Company Scholarship Awards for Excellence for the academic year 2024/5. Pyner's final year project for her degree show in 2025, titled 'On Which We Roam', took its cue from the landscapes of Cornwall, both beneath the soil and under the sea.

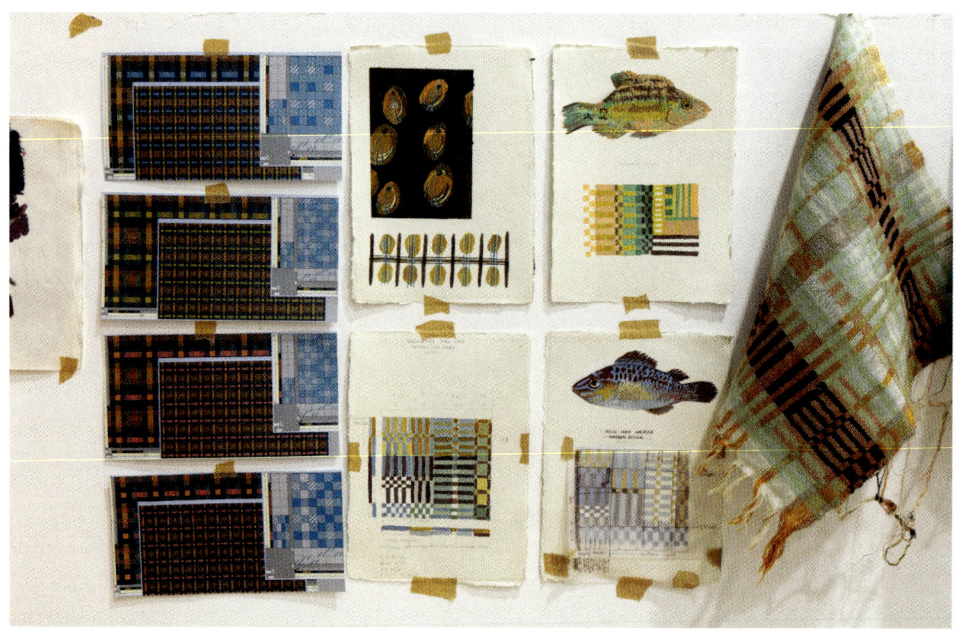

Textiles by Naadia Ahmed-Sheehan, who graduated from Falmouth University in 2024.

Gill says. 'We need to make sure that we are aligned with industry.' Since 2024, students have been offered the option of a third year in industry, before returning to Falmouth for their final year.

'When I graduated in 1993,' says Gill, 'there wasn't much of an industry to go into. There now seem to be more micro-mills opening up and graduate opportunities are increasing.' Falmouth students have found their ways to employers as different as David Walters Fabrics in Sudbury, the Bristol Weaving Mill, Heathcoat Fabrics in Tiverton, and Vanderhurd in London.

CHAPTER 7

Studying Textile Design (2): Technique

In this chapter we look at three more university courses with varying degrees of emphasis on the technical aspects of textile production. Two of them (De Montfort and Central St Martins) integrate design, technical knowledge and production skills, while the new BSc course at Leeds, established in collaboration with industry in 2024, has placed technology rather than design at the heart of the syllabus in order to prepare graduates for more technical careers in textile manufacturing and the wider sector. Although these universities are the subject of a separate chapter, the differences between them and the four we examined in Chapter 6 are not clear-cut – except in the case of Leeds. Generally, the philosophy of good design leading to better business still holds good, particularly in fashion and interiors. Even the most 'creative' courses are aimed squarely at the world of employment.

De Montfort University

'Leicester clothes the world.' The truth of this claim, founded on flourishing industries in knitwear, corsetry, hosiery and shoes, is reflected in the city's Victorian and Edwardian buildings; elegant, imposing, solid, they exude prosperity and confidence.[90] And although Leicester ceased to 'clothe the world' in the last quarter of the twentieth century, the city's fashion and textile tradition has been kept alive by progressive local businesses such as Shahtex (knitted fabrics) and the retailer Next, as well as by the presence of a lively School of Design Innovation at De Montfort University.[91]

De Montfort was established in 1992. Before that it was known as Leicester Polytechnic, which had been formed thirty years before following the merger of Leicester Technical College and the College of Art and Design. The origins of all

these institutions was the Leicester School of Art, founded in 1870 to supply the local fashion and textile industry with skilled designers.

The campus is on an attractive site on the edge of the city, its buildings set out around wide lawns and piazzas, with students walking and chatting over coffee at outdoor tables. The School of Design Innovation is housed in the steel and glass Vijay Patel Building, named after one of Leicester's most successful graduates, a pharmaceutical entrepreneur and philanthropist. This is the home of Footwear Design, Contour (corsets, lingerie, underwear), Fashion, Textiles, Architecture, Interior Design, Product Design and Design Crafts (glass, metalsmithing, jewellery, and ceramics), Photography, Video and Fine Art. It includes exhibition spaces, fashion studios, textile workshops and technology labs.

Professor Carolyn Hardaker, head of the School of Design Innovation, characterises the BA course in textile design as 'thinking forward', with a strong culture of making. It embraces digital design technology, social and environmental responsibility and the worldwide history of fabric design, while never losing sight of its ultimate purpose, to prepare students for working life. 'We are keen that everyone should succeed, and we try to help our students be realistic.' An important part of this is opening their eyes to the multiplicity of careers and roles available in the fashion and textile industries. 'We tell them to have an open mind. We have a fantastic placement unit. They have sent students to materials development firms, design studios, specialists in fashion communications, styling, events... There's a sense of community too, so we have graduates returning to give talks to the students. Three of them work for Margo Selby, another went to New Balance, and another is a consultant in sustainability and innovation for companies in the Midlands.'

The Textile Design department at De Montfort University.

Instructions for creating a full drop pattern repeat (tutor display in Textile Design, De Montfort University, 2025)

The first year of the Textile Design course begins with 'drawing, mark making, just freeing them up'. Then comes a practical introduction to the four main production modes – print, weave, knit, and mixed media. Trying out the various forms of textile production 'helps them decide which areas they can be successful in and where to focus their projects'. In the second and third years, students concentrate on their chosen field, creating a personal collection of work for fashion, interiors or lifestyle. 'Throughout the module they are actively encouraged to compete in national competitions and live projects to further their career prospects and enhance their creative skillset... Placements in industry follow.'

Communication between the different disciplines and branches of knowledge – an essential component of a good university – is lively and continuous, helped by the design of the Vijay Patel Building. There is an easy flow from one department to another, so that students of Contour, Footwear and Textile Design are aware of one another's work and the disciplines that are taught. The equipment is modern and in constant use. We are guided around by two of the staff, Pasqualina Iarrobino and Buddy Penfold, whose expertise and enthusiasm for the task of educating young designers seems to be limitless. This goes far beyond the bureaucratically determined parameters of the job. 'It's really varied and really satisfying,' they say. The students are clearly enjoying themselves and deeply absorbed. Every workstation, cutting table, colouration lab, fabric printer, sewing machine, loom and design desk is occupied. Colourful and exciting work is on display. There is not a mobile phone in sight.

As for the technical/design divide, Buddy Penfold says: 'I don't think there's a problem. For gold standard design you've got to really understand the technicalities of what you're designing. We spend our lives guiding students: "Why not try it like that?" That is born of having worked technically. I worked for years at Coats Viyella producing knitwear for Marks & Spencer. You cannot untangle design from the technical side... We have a really good connection with industry and lots of industry projects throughout all the courses, working with Primark, Crown Derby, Habitat, Lounge, Next, John Lewis, Amtico, adidas Originals, New Balance, John Smedley – lots of different market points that students are exposed to, and these companies want the highest level of design – no compromise in any way.

The university also offers a one-year postgraduate Master of Science in Sustainable Textile Technologies, 'fusing design with technical understanding in the research and development of high-performance and innovative textiles'. Graduates from this course have gone on to work in sportswear and performance textiles, product development and fashion buying, and in regulatory and sustainability roles at companies including Heathcoat Fabrics, Asda, Next, Gymshark, Baltex, Hugo Boss, Finisterre and Rohan. Graduates also go on to PhD study at De Montfort University within the Textile Engineering and Materials Research Group (TEAM), led by textile chemist Professor Jinsong Shen. TEAM has secured research council funding for projects developing new eco-friendly textile processes and sustainable materials. Examples of these include the use of laser technology to apply dyes directly to fabrics (requiring less energy, water and chemicals than conventional methods), and the development of enzyme-based biotechnology to recover valuable resources from wool blended fabrics for recycling and reuse.[92]

Central Saint Martins

Central Saint Martins, part of London's University of the Arts, was formed in 1989 from the amalgamation of Saint Martin's School of Art, founded in 1854, and the Central School of Art and Design, founded in 1896. The Textile Design BA enjoys enormous prestige, owed partly to its location and history, but also to textile artist and designer Philippa Brock, who taught there from 2001 to 2023. Brock brought two leading principles to CSM: first, that students must learn to talk about their work; and, second, that they need good technical skills in order to be able to apply their creative ideas.

The current head of department is Stephanie Rolph, who graduated from CSM in 2013. A winner in 2014 of a Worshipful Company of Weavers' scholarship while studying for her MA at the Royal College of Art, she has collaborated with businesses as various as Hugo Boss, Alexander McQueen, Marc Jacobs, Nokia, Jaguar Land Rover, Jaeger and John Boyd Textiles. With 'A' levels in maths, further maths and physics, as well as textiles, she was always drawn to constructed (knitted or woven) rather than surface (embroidered or printed) textiles. The Textile Design BA is taught in the magnificent workshop spaces of The Granary, the main campus of the college, among the former rail yards, sidings, and warehouses north of King's Cross Station. With about eighty students a year taking textile design, up to thirty might opt for weave.

The course offers a choice of three pathways – weave, print, and knit. What distinguishes its offering is that students drop one specialism after the first term but then keep two running for another three terms, until they are halfway through their second year.

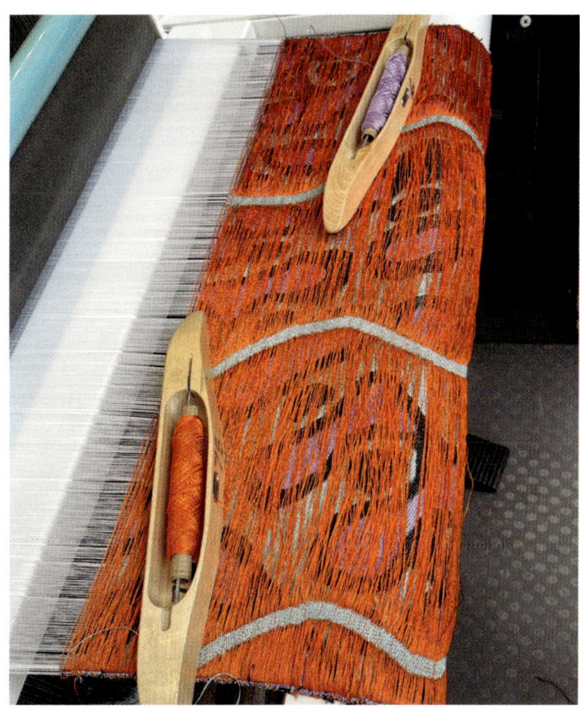

Student work on a TC2 digital Jacquard loom, Central St Martins (2023).

'Thicker than Water' by Catarina Riccabona, a configuration of nine panels created
for the 8 Holland Street Gallery, London, in 2024. Through a variety of textures,
techniques and visceral colours these handcrafted paper-yarn and wool 'tapestries'
explore themes of connection, difference, and the rough and the smooth in family
relationships. Riccabona studied Textile Design at Central Saint Martins. She
is based in Dorset, hand weaving for interior designers, curators and private
collectors. 50 x 70cm per panel, overall c. 150 × 210 cm.

Rolph says, 'It helps with employment that the students have more in-depth knowledge of their second specialism.' Once the choice of specialism is made, students undertake four projects of four or five weeks, including one group project. There might also be a project working with industry. The college has collaborated with a variety of businesses and institutions, including Kirsty McDougall's ReWeave project, Anthropologie, the British Library, DAKS, Dashing Tweeds, Gainsborough, Lego, Swarovski and the Wellcome Trust.

Students are encouraged to take a strong interest in the dyeing rooms to develop their colour accuracy. Rolph emphasises the range of technologies students have access to – from the hands-on dobby looms to the Jacquards, to which students are introduced at the end of their second year, supported by a technical team of three.

On the day we visit, one Jacquard is being used to create a complex three-dimensional weave with an abstract colour pattern. The second is producing a quite different figurative weave inspired by British rural life. Rolph notes,

Weaving studio, Central St Martins (2023).

'You need an intimate understanding of weave structures to be able to programme the Jacquard. Even for a Jacquard designer in a mill, who spends most of their time on a computer, knowing how yarns move is invaluable.'

While students are not assessed strictly on their technical expertise – how skilfully they use the machines – they are assessed on their understanding of what the machines can achieve and how that potential can be stretched to express new design ideas. All final year projects begin with primary research: the journey to develop a colour palette, a structure, a texture, and then produce a woven fabric. Rolph wants her students to feel confident that the skills they learn along the way, including forward planning, project management and patience, are useful whichever area of work they will enter.

Part of Rolph's role is to educate her students about the textile industry. There are ten to twelve visiting lecturers each year, including speakers from various industries: automotive, medical, aerospace, interiors.... The course champions experimentation and innovation, but Rolph is also concerned to ensure a good basic level of competence. Recent graduates include Gabriella Timanti, currently assistant designer of Woven Textiles at Alexander McQueen, and Elaine Yang Lin Ng, who was at Nissan before setting up The Fabrick Lab in Hong Kong. Lara Pain won Young Weaver of the Year in 2023 and runs her own studio weaving textiles for luxury residential and commercial projects, while Ciara Crossan is now head of creative and transport at Camira Fabrics. Distinguished older alumnae include Harriet Wallace-Jones and Emma Sewell of Wallace Sewell, and artist-weaver Ptolemy Mann.

University of Leeds

The Lancashire weaver David Collinge was the driving force behind the BSc in Textile Innovation and Sustainability at the University of Leeds, which enrolled its first students in September 2024. 'I've been bashing on for several years about the need for more textile technology training in the UK. And now, finally, we've got there. As an industry, we are not short of designers, but there hasn't been an undergraduate textile technology course in Britain for twenty years. Everybody in the industry has been saying we need textile technologists, and the universities did previously offer these courses, but they couldn't get any students to enrol on them. So there has been a mismatch, nobody being able to quite put it together.' Recently, he set about gauging interest in a course of this kind, garnering support

Leeds University: buildings contributed by the Clothworkers' Company for the Department of Textile Industries in 1874.

from manufacturers and educational institutions, before approaching the UK Fashion and Textile Association (UKFT) and the Textile Group of the London Livery Companies for sponsorship.[93]

Leeds seemed a good choice for a course of this kind, although Huddersfield University, with its Technical Textiles Research Centre, its excellent facilities and partnerships with local industry, was also a strong contender. The Department of Textile Industries at Leeds, established in 1874 as part of the Yorkshire College of Science, later became a founding department of the University of Leeds. From the mid-1920s it has been deeply engaged in scientific textile research and its strong science and technology roots continue more than one hundred years later, with a large academic and research student cohort, working across polymer and fibre science, sustainable textile manufacturing, dyeing and finishing, nonwovens and technical textiles.

Fabric testing machinery at the University of Leeds Institute of Textiles and Colour.

It has long had the support of the Clothworkers' Company, who paid for the suite of buildings around which the college developed. 'Even before the University of Leeds existed, the Department of Textile Industries was teaching the fundamentals of textile manufacturing,' explains Stephen Russell, Professor of Textile Materials and Technology and Director of Leeds Institute of Textiles and Colour (LITAC) formed in 2001. 'Textile Industries was one of the founding disciplines of the University when it was founded in 1904. After the Yorkshire College of Science opened in Leeds in 1874, we were teaching day and evening students from the local mills, providing formal education, including instruction on the loom and woollen and worsted manufacture. Wool processing was the primary focus, but of course, over time, interests widened to include dyeing, fibre science and many other aspects of textile technology. Looking back to those early days, textile teaching in Leeds started because of a pressing need for technical education and innovation to support industry, and that is a need that continues today.'[94]

Muhammad Tausif is Professor of Sustainable Textile Manufacturing and interim head of the School of Design at Leeds. He describes how, when the working group started to plan the new programme, they carried out an industry-wide survey with retailers, fashion brands and textile manufacturers to identify what skills were lacking within the graduate pool. It emerged that technical skills are most urgently needed. 'If you don't understand the manufacturing processes, from fibre up to the finished product,' he says, 'then how can you know if your design will translate into a functional product? It becomes imaginative rather than meaningful.'[95]

'If you understand how fibre properties and textile structure affect the performance of final products, as well as how to use textile processes as tools to modulate these parameters,' says Stephen Russell, 'then you have the capability to innovate, and engineer textiles for a variety of different markets, which you can't do if your focus is purely on appearance and aesthetics. Whether we're talking about fashion or technical textiles, a deep understanding of the relationships between textile processing, textile structure and textile performance is crucial. Producing sustainable textile products, with quantifiably reduced environmental impacts, also depends on understanding the complex interplay between textile materials, manufacturing and performance'.

Today's university courses are offered in a competitive marketplace, so finding the right name for this one was important. 'Innovation and sustainability' was chosen to appeal to prospective students, with 'innovation' clearly representing the technical character of the subject, and 'sustainability' addressing the concern that many students have with environmental objectives such as reducing carbon emissions, using clean energy and minimising waste. Stephen Russell is quick to point out, however, that there is a lot more to this subject than meets the eye. 'It's easy to overlook the complexities of sustainability, and the technical realities regarding materials and manufacturing. To give an example related to sustainability, a student might say, "I don't want to use polyester (PET) derived from fossil fuels, I want to use cotton." Yet, despite one being a natural fibre, both

The raw material of polyester yarn
Leeds University textile laboratories.

have significant environmental impacts at every stage of the lifecycle, depending on how and where they are produced, as well as quite different physical and chemical properties, which affects the performance attributes of the finished product. These are the sorts of issues that are often overlooked; it's not at all straightforward.'

'Technology is the key enabler,' says Tausif, 'for both sustainability in manufacturing and for driving innovation. We want to be clear with our students that this is a BSc programme with a specific technical focus.'

Conclusion

A visit to any of these universities is an eye-opening experience. The excellence of the facilities, the expertise and enthusiasm of the teaching and technical staff and the liveliness and ingenuity of the students' work are all immensely impressive. So too is the vast programme of industry placements and exchanges.

Looking back at the founding ideals of the art colleges – which were created to improve the design standards, and hence the competitiveness, of the UK's textile trade – we might ask if they have achieved what they set out to do. For half a century or more the answer would appear to be entirely positive. From the mid-nineteenth century to the First World War, Britain was the world's leading exporter of cloth, with approximately half of the global textile trade. However, its share has shrunk dramatically since then, as other countries with cheaper labour costs have industrialised and Britain's imperial power, with its trading privileges, has receded. By 2023 the UK's share of the global textile trade was only 0.84 per cent.[96] While it seems possible that the high quality of design training kept British companies competitive for much of this time, it is clear that global economic forces have inevitably prevailed.

There is, however, a brighter side to this story. Since the 1980s, companies within the UK have adopted a strategy of higher value and lower output, prioritising quality of design, strength and durability of materials, flexibility, service, innovation and sustainability. This could surely not have happened without a rich reserve of talent, well trained and keen to innovate – and, of course, businesses willing to invest and employ. The results are encouraging: the last twenty years have seen the development of micro-mills and design studios, and the revival of woollen, linen and silk mills focused on a luxury market. Another UK area of excellence is in the development of technical fabrics, whether for use in the medical, automotive or airline industries. Exports are rising, and there is a real sense of optimism in the air.

A wall-hanging from 'The Hepworth Collection' by Niamh Weaver, who graduated from Falmouth University in 2024. The collection is inspired by the work of the sculptor Barbara Hepworth. Each piece is 1 metre wide, hand woven using linen and copper.

CHAPTER 8

Alternative Pathways

Weaving is fundamental to human civilisation. Throughout history it has been a primary skill – like cookery or making pots. As a craft, it has also underlain some of our most artful creations – from costumes to rugs to tapestries. For millennia weavers were a highly visible thread in our social fabric, with the skill passed down through families. Whole communities grew up dedicated to the craft and its attendant activities – sheep rearing, spinning, dyeing, carding, cloth-working and so on. Industrialisation changed all that. The making of cloth in Britain became concentrated in a few centres, with fewer people responsible for producing more cloth. For many, how fabric was made became a mystery. And so weaving, as a career, for most people, required making an active choice, rather than responding to an obvious necessity.

Since the nineteenth century it has been recognised that this poses a challenge to the UK's still vital industrial textile sector. As earlier chapters have revealed, the founding of schools of Art and Design from 1837, alongside the founding of the more technically orientated schools and colleges – the Department of Textile Industries in the newly formed Yorkshire College of Science in Leeds in 1874, funded by the Clothworkers' Company, for instance, and Bradford's famous Technical School opened in 1882 – have sought to create educational pathways into the industry for a range of different people with different aptitudes. These have evolved into an array of courses available at universities and colleges of higher education up and down the country, many supported by the London livery companies. But as shall become clear in this chapter, formal education is just one of many educational pathways. And, indeed, even when the primary anchoring is a particular degree, education in weaving spills out to encompass teaching much earlier on, in schools as well as the home, and also much later on, in formal and informal educational settings open both to weavers and aspirant-weavers throughout their lives. The plenitude of

Bernardino Pinturicchio: *Penelope and the Suitors* (about 1509). This picture was painted for the palace of the ruler of Siena in celebration of the marriage of his son. Weaving is key to the story shown. It is the episode from Homer's Odyssey when Odysseus returns from his travels after twenty years of fighting the Trojan War and other trials, to find his wife Penelope besieged by suitors. She has held them off by vowing that she will only remarry once her weaving is complete. Every night she has unpicked the work of the day to ensure that that moment never arrives. The figure who has entered the room carrying a staff – a symbol of a traveller – is probably Odysseus. His ship can be seen through the window. On his return, he kills the suitors with his bow and arrows. As a weaver, Penelope is an emblem of marital constancy and resourcefulness. (Fresco transferred to canvas. 125.5 x 152 cm. National Gallery, London.)

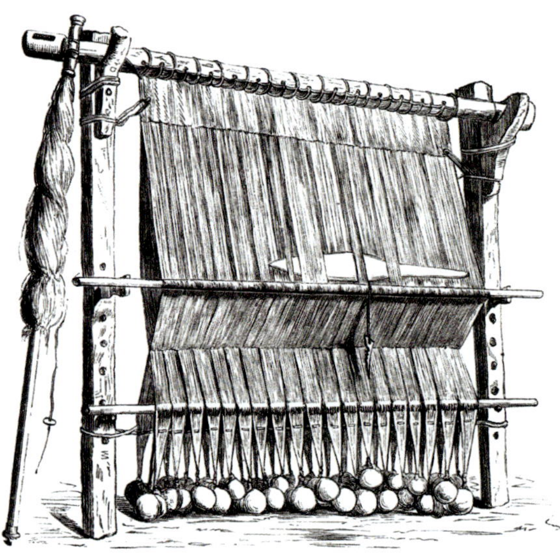

opportunities, mostly a response to continuing demand, is evidence that as well as our constant need for fabrics of all kinds, weaving holds a perennial fascination for the human mind: digital abstraction in a marriage with hand craft.

One-to-one

Perhaps the most old-fashioned route is that discovered by Minnie Hooper, who is two years into her new life as a weaver of Harris Tweed. Hooper spent thirty years working in hospitality, the last ten in Brighton. Both she and her husband had long nurtured a plan to move to Scotland. When in 2021 Hooper's last employer, Bellerbys College, a private school, in Brighton, closed, they took their family of three children and relocated to the tiny village of Marvig on Lewis, in the Outer Hebrides.

But what was Hooper to do? She had read about Harris Tweed and thought that weaving seemed something she would enjoy doing, but with no background in textiles, she had no idea how to set about it. 'One autumn day I was looking through the local paper and there was an ad from the Harris Tweed Authority (HTA) inviting people to apply for a training scheme,' Hooper recalls.[97] Kelly Macdonald, operations manager at the HTA, explains that her organisation is responsible for overseeing the Harris Tweed trade mark. Since the passing through Parliament in 1993 of the Harris Tweed Act, the HTA ensures that all certified Harris Tweed cloth is woven on Harris or Lewis, using yarn supplied by three independent mills, who also finish the cloths returned by the weavers. All Harris Tweed is handwoven on a treadle loom at each weaver's home on a 'double-width' Bonas-Griffith rapier loom, in the case of weavers affiliated to a mill, or, in the case of independent weavers, more usually on an older 'single width' Hattersley loom. The HTA also oversees training, because unless there are people prepared to take on weaving as a profession, on the islands, the mark will die out.

Macdonald explains that while, for centuries, the main educational route had been through the family, in the home, in the 1980s and 1990s there were college courses on the islands to train a new generation. Especially during the 1990s, when new Bonas-Griffith looms were introduced, there was, Macdonald suggests, 'Lots of money for training.' Since then, there has been no college-based training, only a number of different ad hoc schemes and initiatives, sometimes involving group teaching, or sometimes supporting single mentor and mentee relationships. It was a one-on-one scheme that HTA were offering in 2023, when Hooper spotted the ad, with HTA supporting fifteen placements in the homes of fifteen weavers. It was, according to Macdonald, 'massively oversubscribed'.[98] Hooper secured one of the coveted places.

The Harris Tweed Mark, an orb and Maltese cross, first used in 1911. Every piece of authentic Harris tweed cloth is stamped on the reverse with this symbol.

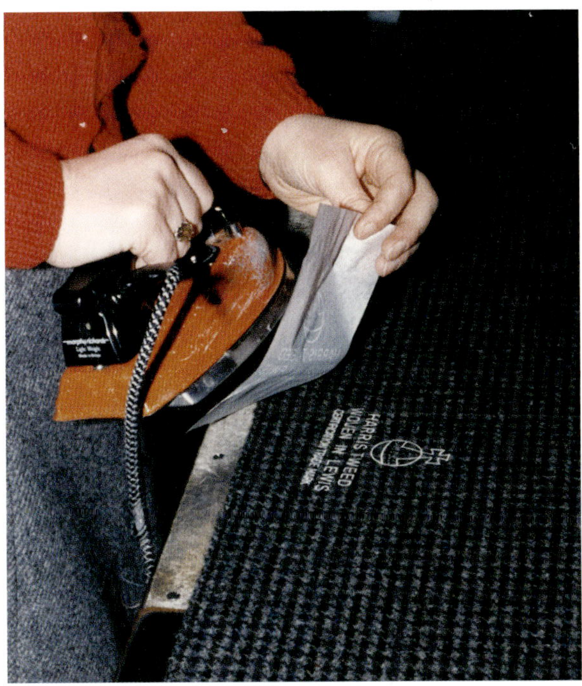

Since one of the criteria for success was that you had a separate workshop large enough for a loom, there is a bias, Macdonald acknowledges, towards older people already established in life. Hooper just had to find a mentor – hard on an island with isolated communities where she knew no-one. But luck and her own outgoing nature led her to the door of Francis Dantinnes, himself an incomer from Belgium, who immediately agreed to teach her on his own loom. Many newcomers to weaving choose to learn the skill slowly, around their other responsibilities, but Hooper was determined to earn her living and repay her £300 contribution to the costs of training as soon as

Minnie Hooper, weaver of Harris Tweed, in her workshop.

possible, so agreed with Francis to study four hours a day, five days a week. She was there for four months. 'I was essentially weaving his cloth. Francis taught me all the techniques and all the loom maintenance. The most complicated bit is dealing with machine breakdowns.' After the HTA had assessed her skills, Hooper arranged to rent a loom from Kenneth Mackenzie Ltd in Stornaway. 'When the delivery men delivered it, they said, "That's it, off you go." It was a daunting moment.' The loom came with a 'test beam', because before Hooper could become an official weaver, she had to produce two test pieces that would meet the mill's approval. It was then that she could sign her contract with the HTA and receive her weaver number. Now she weaves full-time, with the mill delivering the ready-warped beams, huge bags of weft yarn and the pattern cards for the tweeds she is required to make. She says, 'It is a bit hard on the knees and the legs but I really enjoy the skilled work. You are only one of 170 weavers in the world allowed to make this cloth.'

Schools

It took Hooper more than thirty years to find her métier. One of the challenges to the weaving industry is how to impress on young children and adolescents that weaving is not just fun, but can also lead to fascinating, varied and well-rewarded careers. At the time of writing (January 2025) the government is engaged in a review of the curricula for both Design and Technology (D&T) and Art and Design. There are different ways that the idea of textiles can be introduced to children – whether through history, for instance in discussing the Industrial Revolution, or through Design and Technology or even through literature and drama. According to a recent report, *Stitching Together an Understanding of the Barriers and Facilitators to Textiles Education in UK Primary Schools*,[99] there is a wide variety in levels and quality of provision depending upon the particular skills and educational background of the classroom teacher. This research set out to 'establish how much time is spent on textiles teaching, what children learn and make, and whether teachers have the training and resources'.[100] It learned that key barriers include insufficient time, resources and training: 'Teachers reported limited instructional time, with an average of only 7.5 hours per year dedicated to textiles, with 17.6% delivering just one hour annually.' This is part of a broader shift in schools to give precedence to 'core' subjects over creative subjects like textiles. Additionally, 49.4 per cent of participants in the survey stated that they had no dedicated budget for textiles, 'leading many to purchase materials out of-pocket or rely on donations'.[101] In terms of training, the Textiles Skills Centre will use these findings to develop teaching resources to help primary school teachers plan lessons and up-skill themselves. But, as Sarah Tradgett, head of DT: Textiles at Cheltenham College, a co-educational private school, notes, sometimes it is just

A project with Year 3 children at Moreland Primary School in Islington, London, exploring weaving inspired by African textile artists. This was a project led by specialist art teachers provided through the Bow Arts Trust, a London-based charity.

a one-off chance experience that inspires: 'One of my formative experiences was when the Embroiderers' Guild came into my primary school and showed us different embroidery techniques.'[102]

When it comes to secondary education, the picture is similarly patchy, with teachers reporting overall a devaluation of the subject. Since 2014 textiles up until Key Stage 4, or GCSE level, has mostly been taught through the D&T pathway, which has a technical and skills focus, with less room within the curriculum for creative experiment. More recently teachers have preferred to teach textiles at GCSE level within the art and design curriculum, because it is easier to engage pupils' attention and enthusiasm this way – with plenty of opportunity to make. But hours have been cut. Tradgett, who has taught textiles at three different schools,

A child experimenting with a table loom. Weaving can be encountered as part of the Design and Technology curriculum, taking students from primary school up to GCSE level, at the age of 16.

introducing the discipline at St Edward's School, doubling the numbers at John Kyrle High School and Sixth Form Centre, an academy in Herefordshire, before her present position, notes recent government statistics, which show a reduction of D&T: textiles teaching hours for the school year groups 7 to 9 from 5,139 in 2011/12 to 3,325 in 2022/3 and the reduction in the number of teachers for that course from 1,138 to 743, nationally. At GCSE level, the reduction she notes is from 2018/19, with hours of tuition dropping from 4,618 to 3,898 in 2022/3. Teaching staff also fell from 1,262 to 1,029.

The fall-off in teaching of D&T: textiles may partly be made up by teachers choosing to teach textiles through art and design. Rachel Addy, after a career in industrial textiles, including as a fashion buyer, began teaching textiles in schools five years ago, both at GCSE and 'A' level. She has become a passionate advocate for textiles generally – running local not-for-profit networking events for adults for skill sharing and professional development as well as being events planner and a host for the Textiles Skills Centre since April 2021. She is currently head of DT in a state middle school (up to sixteen) in Harrogate. She has recently suggested teaching textiles through a BTEC. She argues that while the D&T: textiles course is useful for its emphasis on pattern-making and technical understanding, the exam paper itself caters primarily to resistant materials, the other option in D&T. The 2025 exam paper, for instance, 'had one question relative to textiles and it was regarding nylon which is a polymer, still associated with resistant materials'. Instead the BTEC fashion and textiles combines technical skills with designing and making. In a competitive global market, it makes sense for students to develop their creative skills, a traditional British strength. While production is returning to the UK, Addy suggests, 'Asian countries still need the British inputs when it comes to design and creativity.'

Getting the balance right is critical for everyone. One of the contributors to the Textiles Skills Centre's 2024 report, *Unravelling The Fabric of Textile Education – Where next?*, Dr. Matthew Taylor of the University of Huddersfield says that students should be made aware of the 'scientific, medical, structural, architectural, mechanical applications of textiles, such as those used in aeronautics and other transportation areas.' He notes military applications – 'camouflage, uniforms and parachutes' – as well as the role of textiles in sports: 'kits to enhance speed, or keep us warmer or drier.' [103] Textile education needs to inspire scientists eager to invent 'new materials with textile properties that use sustainable sources', as well as budding artists, craft practitioners and costume designers.

A textile and fashion class. Textiles can be studied at school and sixth form college through a variety of GCSE, 'A' Levels, BTECS and 'T' Levels. Each pathway places a different emphasis on art, craft, design and technology.

Co-author of the report and founder of the Textiles Skills Centre, Dawn Foxall, is also a forceful advocate for teaching textiles within schools: 'It is without doubt that if we lose textiles as a subject in our schools, we lose life skills we didn't know we needed. We lose the ability to create, make and discover the techniques required to make something unique; make mistakes and realise new methods and ideas; practise fine motor skills and dexterity needed for sewing up a wound or working with fine tools; applications of maths and science to develop new fibres and fabrics to support sports, medicine and space; the patience and persistence to follow a project through to an end product.'[104] She also notes the benefits for mental health and the contribution textile education makes to pupils' understanding of climate change and the circular economy. By becoming more confident in the repair, recycling and reuse of clothing and textile items, children can become active participants in the reduction of waste. As she sums it up: 'We can't lose textiles in our education system.' Over the next few years, the fight for the curriculum and the time and resources to deliver it will continue, but there are plenty of passionate stake-holders determined to ensure that textiles as a school subject and practice survives.

Apprenticeships

If Foxall sees textile education within school as a foundation for life, apprenticeships after school offer a direct route to a living. Since the 1980s the government has supported a variety of different apprenticeship programmes. In 2017, they established the Institute for Apprenticeships and Technical Education, as an arm's-length body of the Department of Education, to work with employers to hone technical education – whether 'T' levels, higher technical qualifications (HTQs) or apprenticeships. They have currently approved a textile technical specialist apprenticeship, at level 4 (equivalent to the first year at university), specialising either in technical weaving or technical finishing, leading to a range of roles within industry. There are also level 2 and level 3 apprenticeships in the textile area, offering a combination of academic study and work for an employer, equivalent, respectively, to 5 GCSEs or two 'A' levels.

One leading provider of apprenticeship training is the Textile Centre of Excellence. Founded as a private, not-for-profit Group Training Association in Huddersfield, West Yorkshire, in 1976, funded largely by seventy-five local textile

Above: Learning on the job: apprentices being trained through the Textile Centre of Excellence, based in Huddersfield.

Right: Shannon Bye is an apprentice weave technician at Whitchurch Silk Mill, where silk has been woven since 1830. She has just completed her apprenticeship with the Textile Centre of Excellence.

manufacturing and processing businesses, they deliver training across a range of industries and sectors. Board Director and Director of Training Martin Jenkins says, 'We have trained around three thousand apprentices over forty-eight years.' Apprentices used to start at sixteen – now they are usually between eighteen and twenty years old. And where the gender split used to be 70–30 in favour of young men, now it is approaching 50–50. The advantage of an apprenticeship is that 'you learn as you earn', Jenkins suggests, as apprentices are taken on by mills and split their time between the workspace and the learning space. He adds, 'We provide training for people to hit the ground running in the mills. It is very different from a university education.' But often, as he also points out, 'those who have been educated through the mill are now running the mill'.

One stellar example is Steven Adams, production director of Wooltex UK, a Huddersfield company specialising in worsted and wool fabrics for public spaces such as hotels, cinemas, banks and cruise ships. Adams explains that while he did well at school, he was bored by it. Aged sixteen, he wanted to leave. So his parents advised him to find some kind of training. By chance, he went to an open day at Huddersfield University promoting apprenticeships, and after talking to some mill managers about what they were looking for, decided to apply. He was offered several, but took the nearest to his home, Camborne Fabrics, down the road at Hopton, Mirfield. He did not know it at the time, but his grandmother had led the weaving team

An apprentice weaver at Camira Fabrics, one of the UK's leading textile producers, based in West Yorkshire. Apprenticeships, a form of training that allows students to 'learn as they earn', were the standard entry to the weavers' trade in pre-industrial Britain, and have been successfully revived in recent years.

at Hopton Weavers, before Camborne bought it. Adams's choice was fortuitous. Camborne was an ambitious and technologically advanced business and has grown into Camira, a world leader in technical and specialist fabrics. The year he began, 1995, the company had just acquired brand new Jacquard looms. 'I was blown away by the technical sophistication of the computerised machines. When I saw rapiers [which carry the weft] for the first time, and saw the speed of the weft insertion, that blew my mind. I had been imagining old wooden looms,' Adams recalls.

Adams was one of four apprentices the year he joined. He quickly excelled, regularly winning Student of the Year awards, and one year winning the Weavers' Company Award, the Woolmen's Award and Young Apprentice of the Year in Manufacturing. By the time he was twenty-two he was running all the warping and weaving in the company, managing more than one hundred people and the creation of £20 million worth of fabric annually. Besides his immediate bosses at Camborne, who encouraged him to take on responsibilities, he credits Dougie Bland at Huddersfield University with motivating him. In 2003, at the age of twenty-

Steve Adams, who began his career as an apprentice with Camborne Fabrics, the predecessor to Camira, working on the looms before he was made company director.

four, he was invited to join the nascent textile company Wooltex UK, which he has helped grow from fifteen looms and one warping machine to a business that does all its own dyeing and finishing, employs 150 people working twenty-nine looms, and produces more than 30,000 metres of fabric each week. Today Wooltex UK's workforce includes seven former apprentices – four men and three women – across different departments within the company.

Late starters

If apprenticeships prepare their students to hit the ground running, there are alternative routes for those who come to weaving later. Majeda Clarke exemplifies some of the challenges that can face weavers in discovering their vocation. She was born in Bangladesh. Her father had originally arrived in Manchester as an eighteen year old to study textile technology, before shifting to a catering course. When eventually he married, and wanted to bring his family to England, Manchester was the obvious destination. Arriving aged five, with very little English, Majeda throve in the state education system. By sixth form, she was being steered towards academic courses, ending up doing both a BA and an MA in English. She explains that although textiles were very much part of her family life growing up – she cites her grandmother's fine Jamdani sari as an inspiration, notes that her mother and aunts sewed and embroidered all their clothes and says that 'colour was how we engaged with each other' – her family wanted her to earn a good living, not 'waste her time' doing an arts degree. 'Schools do not make people aware that there is a world of work for people taking textile and art related degrees,' she suggests.

Majeda Clarke, who took up weaving at age 39 after a career in English teaching and educational consultancy.

Clarke trained instead as an English teacher, rising to head of department before becoming an educational consultant. Together with her husband, she built financial security and had a family. Each time she had a child, however, during her maternity leave, she would allow herself an art evening class. After her third child, she took a textile course at City Lit for a whole academic year, one evening a week: 'I am neurodiverse. I just could not take time off. And I utterly promote lifelong learning.' Her tutor encouraged her to take her talent further, and so, approaching forty, Clarke took the plunge. She undertook a full three-year BA in textile design at the London Metropolitan University – the former Cass School of Art – which allowed her to study part time. Her dissertation, focusing on the political, cultural and economic history of the cotton textile trade and Jamdani weaving, between Bengal and Britain, involved a month's research on the ground in Dhaka. She was awarded a First-Class degree and won the Cass Dissertation Award for her research.

With the mentorship and support of other women – including Clarissa Hulse, Ptolemy Mann and Mary Restieaux – Clarke decided she was ready to set up her own business. She applied to Cockpit Arts and won the Clothworkers' Award in 2016, granting her access to equipment and space. Here she began to build her business. Today she makes three kinds of cloth: ethereal Jamdani muslins in cotton or silk, hand woven in Dhaka by master weavers using a technique that has been passed down the generations and, in collaboration with a small mill in Lancashire, cosy double cloth blankets woven from British wool. With handweaving and dyeing still central to her practice, she also weaves a number of commissioned silk artworks for both public and private clients. For all lines, Clarke

Right: A Jamdani scarf designed by Majeda Clarke: 'Suddenly Towers'.

Below: A selection of blankets from Majeda Clarke's Classical Chroma Collection. Made in Lancashire from a mix of luxury wools spun in the UK, with finishing in the Scottish borders, each blanket comes with a story card and signed card from the mill where it is woven. Clarke writes on her website: 'Classical Chroma tells the story of the ancient Greeks' perception of the colour blue. It's a widely held belief that there is no single word in Ancient Greek for "blue", often evidenced by Homer's description of the sea as "wine dark" and the sky as "bronze". This could be simply poetic metaphor or is it that blue comes in many hues and seems to touch all elements of the colour scale? This collection is inspired by Greece where even the light is infused with blue.'

insists the yarn is traceable and ethically sourced. In their different ways, they reflect Clarke's love of Modernist Bauhaus aesthetics – and exemplify the cross-cultural story-telling that has become the mark of her business. For while she is now primarily a weaver, Clarke is very conscious that her skills as a writer, and her underlying love of literature and history, have supported her work not just in her capacity to write marketing copy but also in her pursuit of textiles that embody narrative. As she puts it, 'People. Place. Environment. That's my thing. I make locally, using local skills, and draw on the dual heritage of my family.'

Clarke is very conscious that her change in direction was made possible by the financial security she had achieved through her twenty-year teaching career and support of her husband. Today she advises on policy surrounding craft education and apprenticeships, and she mentors and supports young weavers, especially from black and minority ethnic communities, to help them achieve their dreams more rapidly.

Tapestry

Curiously, professional tapestry weaving is one sector that draws both young apprentices and older fresh starters. Dovecot Studios in Edinburgh and West Dean Tapestry Studio in West Sussex are dedicated to the painstaking hand production of tapestries designed by artists. This artisan business flourished in the middle

Left: Eileen Agar, *Figures in a Garden*, 1984. This tapestry is a woven version of the surrealist painter Eileen Agar's painting of the same name, dated 1979–81, which is now part of the Tate collection. The tapestry captures the 'deep sensations of time and space' and 'vortex of colour' that artist, collector and champion of the Surrealist movement in Britain, Roland Penrose, noted of his reaction to these paintings.

Below: Elaine Wilson: *Sea View, After JMW Turner.* Tapestry. 2021. Elaine Wilson is a recent apprentice at Dovecot Studios.

of the twentieth century, when artists such as Edward Wadsworth, Sir Stanley Spencer, Edward Bawden, Graham Sutherland, Henry Moore, John Piper and others collaborated with these studios to create rugs and wall hangings. They are currently enjoying a renaissance as renowned artists, institutions and wealthy individuals are again recognising the specific virtues of tapestry as an art form. Though slow to realise, the impact of each artwork can resonate through centuries.

Although officially incorporated in 1946 as The Edinburgh Tapestry Company, Dovecot was named for the sixteenth century dovecot next to its original workshop in Corstorphine, Edinburgh. The studio was established in 1912 by the 4th Marquess of Bute John Crichton-Stuart, who hired Master Weavers Gordon Berry and John Glassbrook from the workshops of his friend William Morris to create two magnificent tapestries for his Victorian Gothic castle at Mount Stuart, Bute. Right from the beginning the studio has hired apprentices to ensure the passing on of this ancient craft.

Today, three of the current team of professional weavers are former apprentices. Their last but one apprentice received some support from QEST – Queen Elizabeth Scholarship Trust – while their current apprentice is partly supported by The Clothworkers' Company. These apprenticeships are all the more important today because the fine art specialism in tapestry that Edinburgh College of Art maintained for many years, under the inspired lead of Archie Brennan, a former apprentice and then creative director at Dovecot, has been scrapped. Naomi Robertson, the lead weaver, asserts that no previous experience is required. In fact, it is easier for her to train people who have never studied weaving than experienced textile graduates. Tapestry weaving is entirely weft-faced, uses no shuttle and the weft is not continuous, all very different from cloth-weaving. She says, 'When they learn the Dovecot way from the start, they're introduced to techniques and traditions that have been passed down through generations of Dovecot master weavers–skills we take great pride in. These methods are essential to maintaining our standards and reputation. I feel strongly about preserving these practices. They were handed down to me when I started at Dovecot, and I see it as our duty to carry them forward.'

Elaine Wilson, a recent apprentice, graduated from Edinburgh College of Art with a BA in painting in 2000. She also studied stitched textiles and Fashion Design at Edinburgh's Telford College, and holds an MA in cultural and creative enterprise from Queen Margaret University, Edinburgh, but the weaving was new to her. While daunted at first by the level of expertise she saw all around her, she has been surprised to find 'I can do that – and actually how quickly it starts to happen'.[105] She works now both on commercial projects and her own speculative pieces.

Right: The headquarters in Sussex, near Chichester, of West Dean College of Arts, Design, Craft and Conservation.

Below: West Dean Tapestry Studio with, in the background, Henry Moore's 1978 tapestry, *Three Seated Women with One Child*. The tapestry studio opened as a commercial workshop in 1976 with a commission from Mary Moore to produce a tapestry from a drawing by her father, Henry Moore. A further seven tapestries were produced in this series.

The West Dean Tapestry Studio is the only other professional tapestry studio in the UK. It was established as a commercial studio in 1976, its first commission being the creation of twenty-three tapestries for the Henry Moore Foundation. Since then, the Studio has worked with a wide range of contemporary artists and designers, including Martin Creed, Tracey Emin and Eva Rothschild, as well as re-creating an important series of medieval tapestries. The Tapestry Studio is attached to West Dean College of Arts, Design, Craft and Conservation, founded in 1971

by Surrealist patron Edward James. Part of its remit is to teach, offering a two-year, part-time foundation diploma in tapestry weaving. The cost is currently £3,006 for two years – a not inconsiderable investment.

Despite its heritage, when weaver Margaret Jones first came to West Dean, the weaving course was not available. As she explains, her route into the medium was more circuitous. Jones had already had a career in complementary medicine, as a reflexologist, but she had never done a degree. Fifteen years ago, she applied to West Dean for a place on their part-time foundation diploma in art and design. The two-year programme involves taking ten short courses in different specialisms. 'From the first day I entered the tapestry studio, I became immediately obsessed,' she says. 'On the Friday night of the first week, I went home and said, "This is what I am going to do for the rest of my life." From then on I saw the world in warp and weft.'[106] Jones was accepted directly from her art foundation on to the full-time graduate diploma in visual arts, without doing a three-year art degree in between, based on her portfolio, scrabbling together money from savings, foundations and grants. Once the two years were up, in 2013, she won a QEST scholarship to continue on to the MFA, specialising in tapestry weaving. Jones now splits her time between teaching, weaving – working on her own projects as well as commercial projects at West Dean – and organising Heallreaf, the biennial international tapestry exhibition she established soon after she graduated. She was awarded West Dean's Valerie Power Prize, for the student who had made the most progress on the MFA course, in 2015, and the international Cordis Showcase Prize for tapestry in 2015. She was one of the weavers on the 2024 Eva Rothschild project for Sadler's Wells East, alongside Emma Straw and Jo Howard, under Studio Lead Philip Sanderson. A late flowering indeed.

A new path

For Graysha Audren, the educational pathway she has chosen has been funded by research grants – an enterprising way to enable experimentation that would have been too high-risk or early stage for investors. Audren began her studies in fashion and textile design at Central Saint Martins in 2016, with a determination to address issues of supply chain and sustainability in the fashion industry. She says: 'There is so much fragmentation in the supply chain and so much waste in the making processes: it can seem quite overwhelming.' In garment production up to 25 per cent of the fabric is wasted in off-cuts and 73 per cent of all textiles produced end up in landfills or incinerated.[107] Her interest in weaving derived from her understanding that here she had a solution to hand. Specialists in printed textiles have no control over the production of their material, but she could see that once she understood the rules governing the weaving process, she would be in a position to experiment not just with the creation of the fabric but also with its future life as fashion. As she puts it, 'I realised I had the power to change the way we make garments.'

Graysha Audren with her WEFFAN loom, programmed to produce not just fabric but garments.

As her third year loomed, Audren knew there were few examples to follow. She had learned about 3D weaving, but to apply that to the creation of entire garments, she would have to invent her own process. Urged on by her tutor, Philippa Brock, she extrapolated from her understanding of double cloth weaving through trial and error, until she was able to produce miniature samples of complete trousers on the CSM's Jacquard looms. The autumn after graduation, in 2019, she showed her work in an exhibition titled 'Seamless' at the London Design Festival, in partnership with Maison/0 – the Central Saint Martins-LVMH creative platform for supporting regenerative luxury.

Details of pockets of trousers woven on the WEFFAN loom.

But where was she to go to learn the next step, to weave real clothes for real people? For the next few years, Audren pursued her quest, supported by Innovate UK, the Young Innovators Programme, and Future Fashion Factory, setting up a research partnership with the University of Leeds and herself plunging into every forum where she could meet UK manufacturers on their own turf and learn from their experience. Rather than paying for a further degree, she used these grants to fund her explorations, setting up her company WEFFAN in 2020.

In 2022 she won the London Fashion District's Design Futures Award, supported by PANGAIA, the materials science company committed to problem solving in the fashion industry. The award was for WEFFAN × Liquid Editions, a collaborative project that culminated in a 3D woven, low-waste outfit that collapses two manufacturing steps into one, merging the weaving of the fabric with the creation of the garment. The innovation operates at the level both of design and of manufacture – and the benefits are in the complete avoidance of waste and the fact

that this process can be accomplished anywhere on an industrial Jacquard loom – meaning that manufacture can be kept local to the fashion brand. As Audren puts it, 'WEFFAN's mission is to be local to the customer.'

Now Audren herself is a conduit for expertise, liaising between fashion brands and mills to ensure that the design and the manufacturing process are perfectly aligned.

Hand weaving

Audren explains that her discoveries have been entirely built upon her expertise in hand and machine weaving processes. She could not have come at her solutions through design or abstract thinking alone. She, like many, fears the consequences for innovation of a depletion of practical skills, as universities are downgrading the practical aspects of teaching in favour of more theory and design. To counter the gloom, however, there are some institutions stepping in to fill the gap.

For many years the Bradford Diploma for Handloom Weaving, taught at Bradford College, was the last formal course to focus entirely on hand-weaving skills (not tapestry). Bradford College is the successor to the Bradford College of Art and Technology, which itself had been formed from the amalgamation in September 1973 of Bradford's Technical College and the Regional College of Art. The Diploma can thus trace its roots back to the original college set up to support the Yorkshire textile industry in 1882. It offered a style of blended teaching – an intensive study period

of a week or so, followed by private study, interspersed with a couple of weekends, and another week at the end of the study – that suited the many older adults who come to weaving after their formal education years, but at a level that could stretch professional weavers as well as inspire amateurs.

When the course was withdrawn, Handweavers Studio and Gallery, now based in Dorset, recognising a need, developed their own. Set up originally in London in 1973 by four friends (Lore Youngmark, Mike Halsey, Raie Barnett and Nancy Lee Child), Handweavers was a shop for yarns, materials and equipment, a gallery and a centre for teaching, serving a wide community of professional and hobby weavers, spinners and dyers in the capital.[108] In 2009 Handweavers was taken on by Wendy Morris and her husband, who moved the centre to the Seven Sisters Road. Two years later, Morris set up the Handweavers Diploma. Today it is run by Dawn Willey and her husband Alan.

Both Morris and Willey were graduates of the Bradford Diploma and wanted to provide a similarly advanced level of practical teaching in a way that could accommodate the needs and commitments of a diverse group of students. 'You can't do a BA part time in any sensible way, but you can do our diploma,' Willey says. Moreover, because they have not sought accreditation by another educational institution, they can be flexible about tailoring the curriculum to the desires of their highly motivated students. The Handweavers Diploma is a two-year course, offered every other year so that there are no overlapping cohorts. Willey limits the number to twelve. As the prospectus indicates, the overall level of core weaving knowledge attained by most students will be 'somewhat beyond the Certificate of Achievement (overseen by the Association of Guilds of Weavers, Spinners and Dyers) and the erstwhile Bradford Certificate in Woven Textile Design'[109]

There is strong demand, Willey reports. The move to Dorset in 2025 has not dinted enthusiasm. As she puts it, 'There seem to have been equal numbers of people delighted the teaching is outside London compared to those who are disappointed it is outside London!' While most participants will be hobby weavers, a number will be professional, seeking to sell their work. As Willey says, 'There is a good appetite for weave, and these courses are becoming ever more important as some universities are losing their looms.' Indeed, one difficulty they have is finding tutors with the right practical skills. Even among graduates of textiles courses with weaving specialisms, there are many 'who cannot warp a loom properly or work out the setts [the number of warp threads per inch] for their projects', Willey says.

While Handweavers offer the only diploma, there are myriad opportunities to learn hand-weaving through short courses, up and down the country, advertised through organisations like the Crafts Council.[110] At the grass-roots level, it seems weaving is thriving.

Saori

At an opposite extreme from a formal educa-tion, through university or an apprenticeship in a mill, is learning to weave using a Saori loom, a technique of freeform weaving that originated in Japan. Claire Hardaker is one of a number of people to have fallen in love with the process, enabling her to combine an interest in textiles with her passion for gar-dening to produce textiles made from natu-ral yarns dyed using locally foraged plants.

Hardaker's original journey into textiles was a conventional one. Born in Bradford, she had been aware of textiles all her life. She studied textiles at GCSE and at 'A' levels. After completing an Art Foundation, she considered doing a textile course at Huddersfield but was put off by the noise and size of the industrial looms. Instead, she took the Costume for the Performing Arts course at the London College of Fashion,

Yarn dyed with camomile by Claire Hardaker, who weaves fabrics imbued with healing plant materials.

before embarking on a career as a costume buyer for the film industry. As she researched antique fabrics and fabrics from other cultures, Hardaker became aware of the 'gap in the level of intention' invested in fast fashion in the contemporary world by comparison with the skill and attention devoted to fabrics in the past.

Ten years ago, Hardaker moved out of London with her young daughter and reorganised her life. She took up gardening and became interested especially in medicinal plants and their healing properties. Simultaneously she discovered the Saori Shed in Diss, the registered Saori weaving studio for the East of England, which promotes freestyle weaving, on a simple Saori loom, with no rules or restrictions. Hardaker says, 'You still have to learn how to warp a loom and the basic structure of cloth', but there is much more room than with a conventional loom for improvisation and self-expression. The loom, she explains, 'is so portable – you fold it like an ironing board. You can carry it anywhere.' As she learned more about the Saori technique, so she also became interested in exploring how to use all the different medicinal plants not just for making dyes but also for creating textile fibres. This is very much slow craft. As Hardaker explains: 'The weaving of a simple shawl might take me twelve hours, but the gathering of the plants and the making of the dyes takes the time.' What inspires her is the idea of wrapping the wearer in healing plant materials, their power enhanced by the care she has invested in the making of each garment.

She divides her time between two-thirds weaving and one-third gardening, ensuring that her work is grounded in the natural world that inspires it. Hardaker also does workshops and goes into schools. She describes a visit to a primary school class of ten- and eleven-year-olds, where one boy she had been warned could be 'a bit of a handful' had absolutely loved the weaving. She reports he had said, 'I can feel overwhelmed really easily and this is the first time I have felt calm at school.' Maybe this was one of those moments, when someone is launched on their life's pathway: as this chapter indicates, the routes are there.

CHAPTER 9

The Worshipful Company of Weavers

During the twelfth and thirteenth centuries, the energies and talents of Europe were gathering in one of civilisation's great bursts of development. Stimulated by commerce, a surge took place in art, technology, building, learning, exploration by land and sea, universities, cities, banking, and credit, and every sphere that enriched life and widened horizons. Those two hundred years were the High Middle Ages, a period that brought into use the compass and mechanical clock, the spinning wheel and treadle loom, the windmill and watermill; a period when Marco Polo travelled to China, and Thomas Aquinas set himself to organise knowledge, when universities were established at Paris, Bologna, Padua, and Naples, Oxford and Cambridge, Salamanca and Valladolid, Montpellier and Toulouse...

Barbara W. Tuchman, *A Distant Mirror*

The livery companies of the City of London are among the oldest institutions in Britain – only the monarchy and the Church are older. They originated as religious and civic 'fraternities' in Anglo-Saxon times, developing after the Norman Conquest of 1066 into guilds or associations of workers in particular crafts or trades.

The guilds, which flourished in towns and cities throughout Europe, had several purposes: keeping up professional standards, training apprentices, setting prices for work, regulating competition, preventing unfair practices, and settling disputes. They also cared for the spiritual and material welfare of their members, and had strong connections with the Church. Each guild had a patron saint and a favoured church or monastery where services would be held and prayers said for the living and the dead. Funerals were highly important occasions, attended by all members. For the old and infirm, financial support or accommodation was provided.

The Priory Church of Saint Bartholomew the Great, Smithfield, founded in 1123, is contemporary with the Worshipful Company of Weavers. The high quality of the building and decorative work suggests an age of technical and artistic accomplishment.

The Lord Mayor's Procession on the River Thames in London, with ceremonial barges of the City livery companies (1747) by Giovanni Antonio Canal, known as 'Canaletto' (1697–1768). Oil on canvas. 122 × 142 cm. Yale Center for British Art.

Each guild was regulated by a governing body known as the Court, with up to four Wardens, a Master (or Prime Warden, or Upper Bailiff), and a number of Court Assistants. A Clerk kept the records and organised meetings, assisted by a Beadle who also played a ceremonial role leading processions and acted as a form of constable when members misbehaved. Craftsmen paid to belong to the guild – the word derives from Anglo-Saxon *gildan*, meaning 'to pay'. As well as subscriptions, the guilds received fines from errant members, payments for apprenticeships and often substantial legacies such as houses and farms.

By the sixteenth century, the London guilds had become wealthy institutions. Fifty-one of them, including the Weavers, had built splendid halls, where courts, meetings, elections and dinners were held, and where legal documents, silver plate and other important possessions could be stored. Their role in the governance of the City of London gave rise to a number of ceremonial obligations and privileges. The right to wear a 'livery' was one of these privileges, exercised on state and ceremonial occasions such as royal visits to the city and the election of the Lord Mayor. Thus, the guilds came to be known as 'livery companies'.[111] In the seventeenth and eighteenth centuries many of these companies built barges for processions on the River Thames: spectacular occasions, with pageants, music, feasting and drinking.

As a rule, there were four classes of members:

- *Apprentices, living with the master's family and learning the trade, normally for seven years.*

- *Journeymen (sometimes known as Yeomen) who had served their apprenticeship and took temporary jobs in different places, but were not yet masters.*

- *Freemen, who had obtained the Freedom of the Company but were not yet full Liverymen.*

- *Liverymen, who had set up in business on their own, were Freemen of the City, and had been admitted as full members of the Company.*

Until the eighteenth century, much of England's wealth was founded on the cloth trade. Several livery companies connected with this trade still exist today: the Broderers (chartered in 1561), Clothworkers (1528), Drapers (1361), Dyers (1471), Girdlers (1327/1449), Gold and Silver Wyre Drawers (1693), Haberdashers (1448), Mercers (1394), Merchant Taylors (1327), Weavers (1155) and Woolmen (1522).[112]

The Worshipful Company of Weavers is the oldest of these livery companies.[113] The exact date of its founding is unknown, but it was certainly in existence by 1130, when the royal exchequer recorded a payment of £16 from the Weavers of London. This was their 'ferm' or annual tax, and it signified a recognised organisation, capable of collecting subscriptions. In 1155 the Weavers received a royal charter under King Henry II, attested by his chancellor, Thomas Becket.

The background to this charter is intriguing. After nineteen years of civil war, the newly crowned king, Henry II (1154–1189), was determined to lay the foundations of sound government. Henry encouraged organisations that were prepared to uphold the law, enforce high standards of work and produce revenue. The grant of a royal charter to the Weavers of London, in the first year of his reign, suggests that they were an important element in his plan – a building block of civil society.

Charter of Henry II to the Weavers of London, granting them their Guild, with the liberties enjoyed in the time of Henry I, and protection from interference in their trade. [1155-1158]. Appended is a fragment of the first great seal of the King. With casts of obverse and reverse.

Charter of King Henry II to the Weavers of London (1155), the oldest existing charter for a London livery company.

The patron saint of the Weavers was St James, and their favoured church was St Laurence Pountney in the City of London.[114] The guild had its own court for pleas of 'debt, contract, covenants and little trespass' and weavers involved in such cases could insist on being tried there rather than in any other court.[115]

The Weavers' aims were generally public-spirited, but their power was resented. They were in continual litigation: with the 'burellers' (finishers and sellers of cloth) who tried to undercut official prices or bend the rules on working hours;[116] with craftsmen who refused to join the guild or pay its charges; with those who kept too many looms or too many apprentices, or taught the craft informally; with tradesmen who arrived from other parts of England or Europe without proof of proper training; and with anyone who tried to cheat their customers or produce sub-standard cloth.

Struggling to control an unruly market was hard enough, but the Weavers also attempted to exercise power over other guilds. This was bitterly resented. 'It is significant,' says one former Upper Bailiff, 'that within thirty-five years [of the Weavers' charter], the other guilds of London had banded together to elect a Mayor (who in effect looks like a spokesman for the other guilds), and that one of the Mayor's first acts was to petition King John for the Weavers' charter to be cancelled.'[117]

In 1202, the king outlawed the guild of Weavers. 'On the petition of the Mayor and our citizens of London, we have granted and by the present Charter have confirmed, that the guild of weavers shall not henceforth be in the City of London, nor be ever restored.'

Fortunately for the Weavers, this revocation failed: the citizens were required to pay twenty marks of silver in place of the Weavers' eighteen marks. The citizens did not pay, the Weavers did, and their guild survived.

Despite this reprieve, the tide of events was against the Weavers. Not only did other textile-related guilds come into being (fullers, dyers, clothworkers, tailors, etc.), but new middlemen appeared: the trader became an important figure and capital a vital factor. Increasingly from the late thirteenth century weavers lost direct contact with the public, as traders supplied raw materials and distributed finished goods – tendencies that affected other trades too and would lead to the decline of the guild system in the sixteenth century.

For much of the fourteenth and fifteenth centuries, while calamitous circumstances such as the Black Death, political instability, murders of kings and outbreaks of civil war made life even more precarious than usual, the Worshipful Company of Weavers was busy defending its members' rights and privileges against

The arms of the Worshipful Company of Weavers, granted in 1490.

Arms:
A blue shield featuring a white/silver chevron, with three red roses on the chevron. Above and below the chevron are three golden leopard heads, each with a gold shuttle in its mouth.

Crest:
A crowned leopard's face holding a gold weaver's shuttle in its mouth, over a silver/red wreath with blue and ermine (white with black spots) drapery.

Supporters:
Two ermine wyverns (winged dragons with two legs), with red tongues and red legs. Their wings are spread wide, showing gold trim and a red rose on each wing.

Motto:
Weave truth with trust.

The 'Inspeximus' of Queen Elizabeth I, confirming the authenticity and validity of the Weavers' Charter in 1559. Inspeximus is Latin for 'we have inspected'.

The 'Inspeximus' of King James I, dated 1604, confirming the Weavers' Charter.

outsiders and rivals. King Edward III (1327–1377) invited weavers from Flanders to settle in England with the aim of improving the quality of English cloth. In 1331, for example, the King issued a letter of protection to John Kemp of Flanders, weaver of woollen cloths, on the understanding that he was to come with his men, servants and apprentices 'to exercise his mystery and to instruct and inform those who wished to learn from him'.[118] The Flemish weavers, threatened with the suppression of their guilds at home, were happy to accept the English king's invitation. Edward's queen, Philippa of Hainaut, was Flemish, and energetically promoted their cause.

Trouble quickly arose. Violence against foreign weavers led to reprisals. In 1362 the mayor 'forbade Flemings, Brabanters and Selanders to carry arms or a knife', and in 1369 a ban was issued on 'hurt or insult upon the men and merchants of Flanders'. Yet the resentment never ceased. In 1380 the foreign weavers were granted exemption from membership of the Weavers' guild, which led to more conflict, appeals, proclamations and agreements. The trouble raged on until 1497, when the English and foreign weavers in London united in the face of rivalry from weavers in other parts of the country.[119]

Despite this 166-year battle, the Company held firm and even prospered. It was granted its arms by the Royal Heralds in 1490, and on 22 December 1498 it bought two tenements in Basinghaw Lane (later Basinghall Street), in the parish of St Michael in the City of London, 'for the wealth and behalf of the said craft for evermore'.[120] Parts of these tenements were rented out, parts adapted for use as a hall over the next half century.

Membership, however, was declining, and money started to run short. By the time of King Henry VIII (1509–1547) the Company's income – from subscriptions, fines, rentals and fees – was insufficient to pay its 'ferm'. In 1546, supplications were made to the King's Council, pointing out that the Weavers no longer enjoyed their original powers, while continuing to pay an exceptionally high ferm. The King, 'in consideration of the then poverty of the same Guild or Company, was graciously pleased to discharge and abate' £12 of the yearly rent of £13 6s 8d.

The Company now began to prosper again, partly through lighter taxation, partly through growing membership and the stimulus to the weaving industry brought about by their old enemy, 'the foreigners'.[121] Membership of a livery company brought advantages to anyone doing business in London, a city that under Queen Elizabeth I was about to enter a golden age.

Over thirteen years (1550–63) the Weavers built a handsome new hall in Basinghall Street, furnished with tables, cupboards and benches, adorned with brightly coloured banners and streamers and 'hangings of the story of Joshua about the hall'. The buttery had an old ship's chest barred with iron, where armour and silver spoons were stored, and the kitchen and pantry were equipped with spits, trestles, racks, platters, pewter dishes, pint pots, salt cellars, saucers and further supplies of arms. Documents and money were stored in the Masters' Parlour, which also served as the Company's business office, while other rooms held stocks of table linen, cushions and – as part of its obligations to the city – fire buckets, wheat and gunpowder. The hall stood in its own garden. 'With such a centre,' writes the Company's first historian Frances Consitt, 'the Weavers could feel that

The interior of Weavers' Hall, Basinghall Street, built to replace the one destroyed in the Great Fire of London (1666). This Hall was replaced by an office building, also called Weavers' Hall, in the mid-nineteenth century, which survived until the 1960s.

they were equipped for all branches of their activities and take pride in the "good, handsome, large building", which justified their heavy expenditure'.[122]

A second influx of skilled craftsmen from abroad occurred after the St Bartholomew's Day Massacre of 24 August 1572, when Parisians rioted against the Protestants in the city (known as Huguenots) killing an estimated 5,000 in a murderous rampage that lasted several weeks. In 1598 the French King Henri IV tried to calm the religious conflict through the Edict of Nantes – a charter of religious tolerance – but this was increasingly ignored as the seventeenth century progressed. The Edict was finally revoked by King Louis XIV in 1685, prompting a renewed Huguenot exodus.

The Huguenot weavers congregated in the Spitalfields area of London – close to the City, but outside its jurisdiction. Attempts were made to keep the 'strangers' from practising their craft, but there was no arguing about the quality of their work. Within a generation they were absorbed into the community, and into the Worshipful Company of Weavers, to everyone's benefit. Several Huguenot families remain connected with the Company to this day, and the Huguenot legacy remains visible in a series of fine houses in the streets of Spitalfields.

Disaster threatened the City of London three times in the seventeenth century: the Civil War (1642–51), the Great Plague (1665) and the Great Fire (1666). During the Civil War, the Weavers, although divided in their loyalties, were required to contribute money, weapons and men – at first for the King, later for Parliament – and had to borrow money from their members to avoid insolvency. Weavers were pressed into service for the defence of London, and the Hall was requisitioned as a tax office and administrative headquarters by the Parliamentary army. Apprentices were called up to fight[123] and, in a brief flowering of democratic enthusiasm, the 'commonalty' were given the right to elect 140 representatives to act for them in the Worshipful Company of Weavers. (After the Restoration, however, this right was seldom exercised and fell into disuse.)

The Great Plague, the worst of many outbreaks of bubonic plague to strike London in the seventeenth century, killed 70,000 in the city over the summer and autumn of 1665. Its horrors were ended the following year by the Great Fire, which destroyed eighty churches, more than 13,000 houses – and forty-four livery companies' halls, including that of the Weavers. The Clerk of that time, James Cole, helped by the Beadle and Porter, saved pictures, boxes of records and ancient charters, and two bags of gold coins worth £400, a daunting task in the crowded and panicky conditions of a burning city. He was thanked with a gift of £50 for his efforts.

Right: Frances Browne, Mrs John Douglas
(1746–1811) painted in 1783/1784 by
Thomas Gainsborough (1727–1788). Oil
on canvas. 238 × 149 cm. The painter, who
was the youngest son of a weaver from
Sudbury, brilliantly captures the beauty
and elegance of eighteenth-century English
silk, while also suggesting thoughtfulness
and delicacy of feeling in his sitters.

Below: The entrance to Weavers' Hall,
rebuilt after the Great Fire of London,
demolished in the mid-19th century.
Watercolour by Thomas Hosmer
Shepherd (1854).

The Weavers set about rebuilding their Hall, completing it in 1669. Shortly afterwards, with a gift of £200 from one of their members, William Watson, they built twelve almshouses in Shoreditch. 'The eastern fringe of London's liberties was ideal for this purpose,' writes the Weavers' historian Alfred Plummer, 'for land was cheap, the situation open and rural, yet the pensioners were not too remote from their friends nor from the Companies' Halls in the City where they had to present themselves to collect their pensions'. A garden was laid out, and Watson added a grant of four sacks of coal to each resident to keep them warm in winter.[124]

The almshouses were part of a pattern of more organised charitable giving, funded by legacies from rich master weavers. In 1618 the Company began paying regular pensions for members, their wives and children, when misfortune, illness or old age reduced them to 'low circumstances'.

Until the Industrial Revolution, the Company retained a measure of economic and social importance, even if it continued to find itself on the losing side in a series of struggles. It did what it could for London's weavers against movements in fashion (such as an eighteenth-century craze for printed calico and chintzes), nineteenth-century liberal economics (allowing cheap imports from abroad) and, most devastating of all, the march of technology and the advent of mass production. As industrialisation and free trade progressed, the Company's power and relevance dwindled drastically. Membership fell from 6,426 in 1736 to 2,613 in 1750, and to 818 in 1810.

Although the nineteenth century saw rapid growth in the English silk industry as a whole, the London weavers failed to keep up with the times. While mills in the North prospered, Spitalfields silk weavers could barely make a living. They became the subject of public concern. Coal cost three times as much in London as in Manchester, and three-quarters of London's looms were idle. 'I have not been able to buy a coat for these five years,' said one of the most skilled of Spitalfield weavers, Thomas Heath, who had to work thirteen hours a day to make a living. In overcrowded, filthy conditions, much of East London languished in poverty and despair. 'Often were we obliged,' said a weaver's wife, 'when half starving, to go without a pennyworth of bread, and buy a pennyworth of coals, or take the children over to a neighbour's to borrow a warm at their fire, or put them early to bed shivering and crying with cold.'[125]

Life for weavers in the North, meanwhile, was scarcely better. Factory conditions were unhealthy, with deafening noise and the air full of fluff that caused respiratory diseases. When textile prices fell, mill owners laid off workers, bringing in unskilled workers from Ireland as well as armed police in response to weavers' strikes. Elizabeth Gaskell described such scenes in her novels *Mary Barton* and *North and South* – still electrifying to read today. As a Unitarian Minister's wife in Manchester, Gaskell knew well the desperate lives she portrayed. Passionate yet fair to both sides, she left her readers in no doubt about the hidden costs of industrial wealth.

In 1838, the year of the Spitalfield testimonies quoted above, a member of the Worshipful Company of Weavers, Samuel Wilson, was elected Lord Mayor of London – the only Weaver to achieve this distinction. An advocate of universal public education and the widening of suffrage, he was a man of strong social conscience. He raised the funds to build new almshouses in Wanstead in 1858–9, with accommodation for twelve men, twelve women and a Superintendent. Wilson's life (1792–1881) 'spans the period in which the hand-loom silk weavers were being "crushed out with infinite misery" and the London silk industry was slowly fading away, while the Worshipful Company of Weavers entered upon the last stage of transformation from an old style craft guild to its modern form as a city livery company'.[126]

The eminence of Wilson highlights an interesting aspect of the Company's culture: 'The Company, with its small number of members, always has a strong family feeling and a substantial proportion of the membership who are excellent in carrying out the good work of the Company in various different spheres, so it is difficult to say that any one member should be thought of as having extraordinary influence.'[127]

These are the words of Jonathan Ouvry, who served the Company as Clerk for twenty-three years (1973–96) and as Upper Bailiff in 2002–3, and whose father Romilly also served as Clerk. When pressed for the names of key twentieth-century figures, Jonathan Ouvry wrote as follows:

I would pick two people to mention particularly, firstly Lawrence Tanner. Tanner was Clerk for forty

The entrance to the Weavers' almshouses, built in 1858–9 in Wanstead, East London. The date on the building (1851) refers to the year when the old almshouses in Porters Fields were demolished to make way for a new road (Commercial Street). Under the foundation stone is buried a copy of the Company's charter from King Henry II, a history of the Weavers' almshouses before 1858, and a list of donors. The company built its first almshouses in the 1670s.

years, ending in 1960 when my father took over, so he covered a period including post-World War I recovery, the thirties when the Company was regarded as a nice gentlemen's dining club, the forties when the Company had to be kept going during the War, and the fifties when the Company was just beginning to recover status and influence. He was an interesting and learned man, combining teaching at Westminster School with being Keeper of the Muniments at Westminster Abbey, where he made many interesting historical discoveries. He was Upper Bailiff in 1963–64.

'Secondly I would mention Geoffrey Reynolds Yonge Radcliffe. The Radcliffe family has been active in the Company for many generations. Geoffrey was Bursar of New College, Oxford in the thirties and during the War, and with Tanner was greatly influential in keeping the Company going and also in introducing new blood. There is still a very strong New College presence in the Company. Geoffrey was Upper Bailiff three times.'

At the end of the Second World War the Weavers were left with a bombed-out office building (their former Hall) at 22 Basinghall Street and some modest charitable activities. In 1947 they purchased 20 and 21 Basinghall Street from the Ironmongers' Company with thoughts of building a bigger Hall.[128] After careful discussion, however, it was decided to abandon the project and sell all three properties in 1961.

Weavers' Hall entrance as it appeared in 1939. Two years later the building was badly damaged in the Blitz and was eventually demolished in the early 1960s.

The Company's fortunes received a spectacular boost in the late 1940s with a bequest from Sir Cecil Bigwood (1863–1947), a lawyer and magistrate who had served as Upper Bailiff in 1911–13. Bigwood left three South London estates to the Company, in Beckenham, Lewisham and Catford. During the 1960s these properties were sold to local residents and housing associations.

With money in the bank, and investments transferred from housing to stocks and shares, the Company's activities blossomed. Another key figure mentioned by Jonathan Ouvry was David Mynors, another New College man: 'David was with Courtaulds for many years, combining a textile connection with his excellent business brain. He was extremely influential in the financial improvement of the Company, being Chairman of the Finance committee for many years, and laying the foundation of the excellent finances that we have enjoyed for many years. He was Upper Bailiff in 1968–69.'[129]

Imaginative and unusual decisions were made. In education, where livery companies had a long tradition of endowing independent schools such as St Paul's, Merchant Taylors' and Haberdashers', the Weavers chose to support primary schools in the poorest areas of London. As well as supplementing meagre school budgets, members of the Company began to serve on boards of governors, meeting regularly with teachers to discuss problems, and helping pupils with their reading. Recent initiatives include buying new tables, funding extra classroom assistants, the provision of speech and language therapists and refurbishment of classrooms and playgrounds.

The three schools currently supported are Grange Primary School in Southwark, St Andrew's in Lambeth and Chisenhale in Tower Hamlets. In an age of declining public investment, the staff of these schools face an unequal struggle. As one former Upper Bailiff puts it, 'What we do is a drop in the ocean… Primary schools are sometimes little more than care projects. Children haven't got enough to eat, teachers help out of their own pockets, which are not deep.'[130]

As an example of the problems that the schools have to deal with, and the help that the Weavers' Company is able to offer, it is worth quoting a report by Peter Baxendell, a governor at St Andrew's in 2025:

> What makes St Andrew's so special is that it focusses not only on spiritual and academic education but on instilling all its pupils with a vision and belief in what they can achieve. As their school song says: St Andrew's strives to be a family, where children are safe and happy, where they stick together; and where children can be confident in who they are.

David Mynors, Upper Bailiff of the Worshipful Company of Weavers 1968–9 and a long-serving and capable chairman of its Finance Committee.

Achieving this positive vision is not easy… Nearly a third of the children have special educational needs, nearly half receive a pupil premium provided for children from the poorest backgrounds. Sadly, there are incidents of children being referred to social care, children requiring a Children in Need Plan, or a Child Protection Plan, or children requiring Special Guardianship. All too often, a child's attendance record or a child's academic achievement is affected by issues outside the school. Sometimes the child is the only person in the household who can speak English. Sometimes the child is the only effective link to social services. To alleviate the impact on their children, St Andrew's extends its safeguarding beyond the school gates, ensuring appropriate social services, health, or police support is in place so that the child's education and wellbeing is not impacted. Last year, the Weavers' provided funding for a classroom assistant to be trained up to support this unique safeguarding service which does so much to ensure the children feel supported and cared for by the school. In addition, the Weavers' fund four Vision Awards and a special Cooper Award (named after Michael Cooper, Liveryman and Governor) which are presented at the end of each year by the Upper Bailiff to recognise children from across the school who contribute to school life by their positive outlook, helpfulness, and kindness.

During the past 12 months St Andrew's has passed its Ofsted inspection with flying colours. As with all London schools, there are far more spaces at the school than children to fill them, which places huge pressure on staff and governors to manage the school's resources effectively, but as with all things at St Andrews, the children always come first so that every child, irrespective of background or circumstance, can like the school motto says 'Reach for the Stars'.[131]

For other charitable projects the Weavers deliberately chose an unpopular field – people serving prison sentences: 'trying to keep young people out of prison, helping people once they are in prison, and helping people once they have come out of prison'. After fifty years in this field, the Company is well known and respected. The Chief Inspector of Prisons, Lord Ramsbotham, was co-opted as an Honorary Member of the Company, and his successors have continued to be deeply involved.

The oldest of the Company's charitable projects is its almshouses in Wanstead. Today the right to live there is no longer restricted to former weavers. Working for the

good of a particular group of craftsmen has broadened into working for the common good. Edward Martineau, chairman of the Almshouses Committee 2015–25, noted in his final report that 'the average lifespan of those living in an almshouse was materially longer than for those who did not', and that the spirit of community, the gardens, the Christmas lunch, Summer Party and other social occasions make the Weavers' House 'a thoroughly life-enhancing experience'.[132]

After the Second World War the Company began to revive its connections with the textile industry. Grants were made to art colleges around the country, for scholarships, materials and equipment, and more recently for an Entry to Work Scheme. This gives financial support to companies taking on young graduates, paying two-thirds of their first six months' salary up to £7,000. Twelve placements are funded each year; most turn into full-time jobs. The Company's annual Woven Textile Design Award, presented at the New Designers exhibition in London, brings new talent to the notice of the industry and has launched many a successful career. Meanwhile significant lifetime contributions to the weaving industry in technology, management, education or the craft of weaving are recognised with the Company's Silver Medal.

A more recent initiative is the Textile Livery Group, set up in 2018 by John Snowdon (Clerk of the Worshipful Company of Weavers 2002–20) to share knowledge and co-ordinate action. The thirteen textile-related livery companies provide funding, and the UK Fashion and Textile Association (UKFT) runs a conference each year for representatives of the textile industry. The first four conferences have been held on the topic of Sustainability.

Looking to the future, the Company is working on new charitable programmes and ways of making the membership more inclusive. This great cause, which had its origins more than a century ago in movements for women's rights and civil rights, has taken on particular public significance in recent years. The Worshipful Company of Weavers began their programme of change in the 1980s with the opening of the Livery to women.

For most of the Company's 900-year existence women weavers were welcomed, and not only as wives, widows and daughters. They could make and sell cloth; they could take on apprentices and were subject to the same rules as men. They were not, however, admitted to positions of power, and at certain times their rights to learn and exercise the trade were restricted. A rule of 1577 states that no silk weaver 'shall kepe, teache, instructe or bringe upp in the use, exercisinge or Knowledge of the same Arte or Mysterie of Weyving any mayden, Damsell or other Woemen

Top: Andrew Stevenson, senior textile designer at Paul Smith, showing fabric samples to two wardens of the Worshipful Company of Weavers, James Early (centre) and Stephen Combey (right). Andrew Stevenson won the Woven Textile Design Award at the New Designers exhibition in 2008 and became a liveryman in 2023.

Above: Freda Newcombe, who was the Weavers' Clerk from 1996 to 2002 and the Company's first female Upper Bailiff (2008–9). In 1987 she and Pat Winterton were the first women admitted to the Livery in the Company's history.

whatsoever'.[133] By the later seventeenth century the restrictions on women weavers had been eased. 'Girls could be formally apprenticed to weaving and the Company would enrol them and in due course admit them to the freedom as they did Anne Archer [in 1703]; but actual examples are few – probably not much more than 1 percent of all apprentices bound at the Hall.'[134]

In the last fifty years the situation has changed profoundly. The pioneer was Freda Newcombe, who was appointed Assistant Clerk in 1971. (At that time the post of Clerk was a part-time activity for a solicitor.) The Company now had a full-time employee and money in the bank, and was able to take on more ambitious charitable projects. In 1975 Freda Newcombe was made a Freeman of the Company, then a Liveryman in 1987. In 1996 she was appointed Clerk, now a full-time professional role equivalent to chief executive officer. She retired in 2002 having served the Company for thirty-one years. She was Upper Bailiff in 2008–9. In more recent years, Rebecca Ridley has been Upper Bailiff (2025–6), and in the 900th anniversary year (2030) the post is scheduled to be held by the designer weaver Harriet Wallace-Jones.

Endnotes

1 The report, commissioned by UKFT, was researched and written by Oxford Economics. The Executive Summary was published on the UKFT website on 14 November 2023. The full report is available on request from UKFT.

2 Even at the lower level, these figures are impressive since the population in England in 1761 was only 6,310,340 (population historians Keith Sugden and Anthony Cockerill: 'The Wool and Cotton Textile Industries in England and Wales up to 1850', in https://www.campop.geog.cam.ac.uk/research/occupations/outputs/onlineatlas/textiles.pdf, accessed 15 January 2026).

3 The minutes from a meeting of the Clothworkers' Company of the City of London in May 1873 state proudly, 'The great demand for fancy woollens of late years has afforded full employment both to pattern designers and to dyers, and the discovery of Aniline has led to vast improvements both in the patterns and colours of the better classes of woollens.' Regina Lee Blaszczyk, *Fashionability: Abraham Moon and the creation of British cloth for the global market* (2017) p. 49.

4 Dr Lauren Padgett, 'Built of Wool: Worsted Collection', Bradford District: Museums and galleries, 21 October 2022, https://bradfordmuseums.org/built-of-wool-worsted-collection/#:~:text=In%20 1900%2C%20the%20Bradford%20 Observer,Bradford%20is%20built%20of%20 wool%E2%80%A6, accessed 15 January 2026.

5 Major names here are Camira, Angus Fire, Heathcoat, and Arville.

6 Interview, 10 March 2025.

7 https://makeitbritish.co.uk/opinion/challenges-facing-uk-fashion-and-textile-manufacturers/#:~:text=Italy%2C%20 Portugal%20and%20Turkey%2C%20 our,UK%20manufacturers%20get%20 very%20little, accessed 14 January 2026.

8 Quoted in Janet Rae, *Fabric of Scotland* (Elgin, 2018), p. 56.

9 This and other quotations from Edward Harrison are taken from a series of newsletters that were published as a book, *Scottish Woollens*, in 1956. This was issued in a new edition by Johnstons in 2016. These words about the First World War are from Newsletter 21 (December 1939).

10 *Scottish Woollens*, Newsletter 22 (April 1940).

11 Janet Rae, *Fabric of Scotland* (Elgin, 2018), p. 93.

12 The report is by DTZ Pieda Consulting, commissioned by the Scottish Executive Enterprise and Lifelong Learning Department (SEELLD) and Scottish Textiles Network. Quoted in Rae, p. 103.

13 Matthew Blair, *The Paisley Thread Industry and the Men Who Created and Developed It* (Paisley, 1907), p. 112.

14 https://alex-begg.co.uk/environment, accessed 14 January 2026.

15 Conversation with the author, 11 October 2023.

16 Conversation with the author.

17 Conversation with the author.

18 James Sugden OBE (1946–2017), 'A Short Video Celebrating the Achievements of James Sugden', www.weavers.org.uk, accessed 15 January 2026.

19 The next largest sector, metal goods, represented only 19 per cent.

20 Saltaire, near Bradford, and New Lanark near Glasgow are the other two. Both are examples of enlightened capitalism, where the owners were determined to prove that it was possible to run a successful factory without mistreating the workers.

21 Queen Street Mill in Burnley (Lancashire County Council); Styal, south of Manchester (National Trust); Leeds Industrial Museum; and Coldharbour Mill near Tiverton are four particularly impressive examples.

22 W. Bennett, *The History of Burnley* (Burnley, 1946), Vol. II, p. 114.

23 Conversation with the author, 11 May 2023.

24 Conversation with the author, 5 October 2023.

25 The exhibition at the Dundee V&A ran from 1 April 2023 to 14 January 2024 and was widely reviewed. See Ben Macintyre, 'My ancestor modelled our tartan when George IV came to town', *The Times*, 25 March 2023, pp. 8–9.

26 Conversation with the author, 9 October 2023.

27 Conversation with the author, 20 August 2025.

28 Conversation with the author, 20 August 2025.

29 'If all barriers to exports were removed, we estimate the fashion and textile industry could potentially support a further £7.6 billion in gross value added contributions, alongside an additional 160,000 jobs and £2.8 billion in tax receipts when compared to the total core economic footprint of the fashion and textile industry. Similarly, if all barriers to workforce and skills shortage were removed, we estimate that the fashion and textile industry could potentially increase the sector's gross value added contribution by £4.7 billion, support another 98,000 jobs, and stimulate £1.8 billion more in tax revenues.' *The Fashion & Textile Industry's Footprint in the UK* (Executive Summary, October 2023), p. 10. UKFT website: https://unbxd. ams3.digitaloceanspaces.com/ukft.org/wp-content/uploads/2023/11/04181525/OE-Report-executive-summary.pdf, accessed 15 January 2026.

30 This is one theory. Another is that the mob was sent in by Heathcoat's competitors in the Nottingham lace industry.

31 John Stimson of Heathcoat Fabrics in conversation with the author, 12 February 2025.

32 PFAS (per- and polyfluoroalkyl substances) are a group of some 10,000 chemicals used in an enormous variety of industrial and domestic applications. Known as 'forever chemicals' because of their extreme durability, they have been traced in drinking water, food, soil, sea and air and are suspected of being hazardous to health. Descriptions of PFAS on the Internet tend to be coloured by political or economic interests. For a view from the European Environment Agency see https://www.eea.europa.eu/en/analysis/publications/pfas-polymers-in-focus (published 29 April 2025), accessed 16 January 2026.

33 Email to the author, 16 September 2025.

34 Conversation with the author, 12 February 2025.

35 Conversation with the author, 18 February 2025.

36 Conversation with the author, 5 March 2025.

37 In a document on the Camira website ('ReSKU 2.0 What You Need to Know') we see this Q&A:.

- Why is textile circularity becoming more important?.

- The textile industry is responsible for a huge amount of waste – globally, an estimated 92 million tonnes is created each year (Source: UCL), while just 1% of material used to produce clothing is recycled into new clothing (Source: Ellen MacArthur Foundation). Even though we are a zero to landfill company, inevitably we create textile waste from our own manufacturing, notably yarn remnants, fabric selvedges and sometimes off-quality fabric. Our biggest source of internal waste is the wool-polyamide yarn remnants from our face to face transport manufacturing in Lithuania. It made sense for us to look to address this waste stream as a priority, which we did firstly with the Revolution fabric, introduced last year. This was a 'proof of concept' development, using 31% recycled content, giving us the learning expertise to push

the boundaries further to include more waste yarn and then blend it with flax fibre from harvested plants.

(https://content.camirafabrics.com/media/nvwnaitl/resku-20_things-you-need-to-know.pdf, p. 2.), accessed 16 January 2026.

38 Conversation with the author, 5 March 2025.

39 Anni Albers, *Pictorial Weavings* (Cambridge, MA: Massachusetts Institute of Technology, 1959), opening page.

40 *Ibid.*

41 For the purposes of this chapter an art textile is one both made and conceived by a single artist. To this day beautiful woven tapestries are created by skilled artisans in studios such as Dovecot in Edinburgh or West Dean College of Arts and Conservation in Sussex, in collaboration with artists who provide a drawing or a cartoon.

42 *Ibid.*

43 As Lynne Cooke writes in her essay 'Modernist histories: Braided, interlaced, and aligned' in the 2023 exhibition catalogue *Woven Histories: Textiles and modern abstraction* (The University of Chicago Press, p. 31): 'The historical avant-gardes viewed the intersection of art, design, and industrially scaled manufacture as critical to shaping a better world. Textiles played a central role in those utopian social visions.'.

44 Ethel Mairet, *Hand-Weaving Today: Traditions and changes* (London, 1939), p. 14.

45 Interview with Peter Collingwood, *Handwoven* magazine, 1987, 14 September 2023,https://inexpensiveprogress.com/6722/peter-collingwood-interview/, accessed 10 January 2026.

46 *Ibid.*

47 *Ibid.*

48 Diane Sheehan and Susan Tebby, *Ann Sutton* (The Crafts Council in association with Lund Humphries, 2003), p. 11.

49 *Ibid.*, p. 8.

50 Email correspondence with artist, 29 September 2024.

51 'Colour is very seductive, and so I tend to use it for identification purposes, to aid understanding, rather than as a cosmetic' (email correspondence, 28 September 2024).

52 https://www.craftscouncil.org.uk/about/history#:~:text=Introduction,and%20

improvement%20in%20their%20products', accessed 10 January 2026.

53 The title Royal Designer for Industry (RDI) is awarded annually by the Royal Society of Arts (RSA) to designers of all disciplines who have achieved 'sustained design excellence, work of aesthetic value and significant benefit to society'. According to the RSA's website, the RDI 'is the highest accolade for designers in the UK'. Only 200 designers can hold the title.

54 *Age of Experience* (Ruthin Craft Centre, 2009).

55 Conversation with the author, 2024.

56 Interview with the artist, 15 July 2024.

57 'The older I get the less I plan. I am really interested in accidental colour and unconscious colour. That is when colour gets really interesting. People always try to control colour, quantify it, and there is a lot of fear around colour. What I have learned is that if you can let go of that fear, really interesting things happen.' Interview with the artist.

58 Interview with the artist, 28 September 2024.

59 She has marked the moment with the 2024 publication of the monograph *Ptolemy Mann: Thread painting* (Hurtwood Press).

60 Interview with the artist, 18 July 2024.

61 Interview with the artist, 25 July 2024.

62 Interview, 25 July 2024.

63 Conversation with the artist, 11 July 2024.

64 As we shall see in Chapter 6, this was a deliberate policy, conceived in the 1830s to improve the quality of industrial design – a policy that has been very successful, and produced such varied long-term benefits to the economy, culture and quality of life of Britain that its value should be beyond question. In fact, it can be argued that it is only because of its exceptional quality of design that a textile industry exists at all in Britain today.

65 London Transport, and particularly the Underground, has a long tradition of commissioning outstanding architects, artists and designers to create visuals for the network: notices, posters, station signs, colour schemes for carriages and fittings.

66 Peta Levi MBE (1938–2008) devoted her life to promoting young talent in design.

While working as a journalist specialising in design and new technology for *The Times*, the *Financial Times* and *House & Garden*, 'she became increasingly aware of a huge British river of design talent that was simply running away. First step to dam the flood was to found and organise the New Designers exhibition…She was an imaginative, indomitable and selfless champion' of young designers (Barbara Chandler, *Independent*, 6 May 2008).

67 Conversation with the author, 22 June 2023.

68 Note to the author, 8 July 2025.

69 'We envision a textile system that embraces the values of decolonised and equitable soil-to-skin processes. We will strengthen an international system of diverse textile communities that directly enhance regional economies for the purpose of generating permanent and lasting systems of localised fibre production. These regional land regenerating production systems will diminish pressure on the ecologically undermined areas of the world.

'We see a nourishing tradition emerging that connects the wearer to local fields where clothes are grown in a system that can last for countless generations into the future. Through a host of scientifically vetted soil carbon enhancing practices, our supply chains will create "climate beneficial" clothing that will become the new standard. We envision a world looking to rapidly mitigate the effects of climate change where consumers, manufacturers, designers, and ecologists collectively rethink and re-imagine the life cycle if garments' (https://fibershed.org/mission-vision/), accessed 16 January 2026.

70 Conversation with the author, 27 February 2025.

71 Conversation with the author, 28 February 2025.

72 A short film about the collaboration, with a performance of Helen Caddick's music at Somerset House, can be found on Margo Selby's website: https://www.margoselby.com/pages/process-film-moon-landing-2024?srsltid=AfmBOorKSBWHJxqHElsR eSzQFEuNTRp6i6Gi7CSO8bPMeUNCj ooRTNdt, accessed 16 January 2026. *Local history note:* Margo Selby, Helen Caddick and the filmmakers (Rich Sound and Vision) all live and work in Whitstable.

73 Conversation with the author, 28 February 2025.

74 Conversation with the author, 26 February 2025.

75 *The Chap* is a semi-serious magazine dedicated to grooming, tailoring and other gentlemanly pursuits, edited and founded by the impeccably dressed Gustav Temple. The Chap Olympiad, featuring such events as sauntering, tie knotting and umbrella jousting, has been held every year since 2009 in London's Bedford Square. Rules are strict: no modern sports clothing to be worn, and 'points are deducted for seeming to be trying too hard'.

76 Conversation with the author, 26 February 2025.

77 Conversation with the author, 21 November 2023.

78 'The Government School of Design', *Illustrated London News*, Vol. 2 (1843), pp. 375–6.

79 H.K. Briscoe, 'The History of Technical Education in Nottinghamshire, 1851–1902', unpublished M.A. thesis (University of Sheffield, 1962), pp. 64–5, quoted in David Wardle, *Education and Society in Nineteenth Century Nottingham* (Cambridge, 1971), p. 126.

80 Stana Nenadic, 'Designers in the Nineteenth Century Scottish Fancy Textile Industry: Education, Employment and Exhibition', *Journal of Design History*, Vol. 27, No. 2, 2014, p. 120.

81 'Moving from a career in design to one in the fine arts was an ambition for many students in the government design schools, and that this happened was a frequent cause of criticism of the effectiveness of such institutions in the great national project of industrial improvement.' *Ibid.*, p. 126.

82 The Athenaeum, 29 October 1836, quoted this extract from the evidence laid before the Ewart Committee, 1835–6. This was quoted in Walker, Vera (1951) 'The Life and Work of William Bell Scott, 1811–1890', Durham theses, Durham University, p. 54. Available at Durham E-Theses Online: http://etheses.dur.ac.uk/1423/.

83 Nikolaus Pevsner, *An Enquiry into Industrial Art in England* (Cambridge University Press, 1937), p. 6.

84 *Ibid.*, p. 53.

85 Quoted from an interview with Christopher Andreae, 'The Christian Science Monitor', 7 August 1990, https://www.csmonitor.com/1990/0807/ptex.html, accessed 10 January 2026.

86 Interview taken during visit to the university, 10 April 2024.

87 This was gutted by fire in 2018 and still under repair in 2025.

88 Helena Britt, 'PRINTED TEXTILES // THE CLOTH // FRASER TAYLOR: Enhancing Access and Utilisation to The Glasgow School of Art Archives and Collections', 2016.

89 Interview taken during visit to Glasgow School of Art, 13 February 2024.

90 'Leicester clothes the world' was announced on the front cover of the *Leicester and County Chamber of Commerce Monthly Journal* in June 1938.

91 Leicester's other university (the University of Leicester) is renowned for its scientific achievements, but this too owes its existence to the textile industry. Its first buildings and land were donated by Thomas Fielding Johnson, a Victorian philanthropist whose wealth derived from a worsted spinning business.

92 One of the TEAM research projects, a collaboration with Loughborough University and a group of textile businesses, is described in more detail here: https://www.texintel.com/blog/texintel-08-24-innovation-spotlight-de-montfort-university-unveils-textile-innovations-to-enable-circularity, accessed 16 January 2026.

93 The UKFT is also addressing this issue through the introduction of its Young Textile Technician Fund, which covers 50 per cent of the costs of training for young textile technicians – with the support of the Weavers', the Clothworkers' and the Drapers' Companies.

94 Conversation with the author, 23 November 2023.

95 Conversation with the author, 23 November 2023.

96 https://worldpopulationreview.com/country-rankings/textile-exports-by-country, accessed 2 January 2026.

97 Zoom interview conducted on 17 January 2025.

98 Interview by phone, 15 January 2025.

99 Roy Ballam and Lynne Mason, *Stitching Together an Understanding of the Barriers and Facilitators to Textiles Education in UK Primary Schools* (Textiles Skills Centre, January 2025).

100 *Ibid.*, p. 5.

101 *Ibid.*, p. 15.

102 Telephone interview, 23 January 2025.

103 *Unravelling the Fabric of Textiles Education* (Dawn Foxall and Roy Ballam), p. 3.

104 *Ibid.*, p. 2.

105 Quote from a video featuring Elaine Wilson as part of the exhibition 'The Art of Being an Apprentice', 3 March–3 August 2021, https://dovecotstudios.com/exhibitions/the-art-of-being-an-apprentice, accessed 12 January 2026.

106 Telephone interview, 16 January 2025.

107 Teleri Lloyd-Jones, 'Machine Ready', 21 June 2019, https://www.arts.ac.uk/colleges/central-saint-martins/stories/machine-ready, accessed 12 January 2026.

108 'About Handweavers', https://www.handweavers.co.uk/about.irs?srsltid=AfmBOoqJDLbO7bO-onkcA57DNG4L2tgov_eJqOJnQxnV7-zuCRIHoxN1, accessed 12 January 2026.

109 'The Handweavers Diploma 2025–2027', https://www.handweavers.co.uk/diploma-prospectus-2025-2027.irs, accessed 12 January 2026.

110 Laura Snoad, 'Where You Can Learn to Weave in the UK', https://www.craftscouncil.org.uk/stories/where-you-can-learn-to-weave-in-the-uk, accessed 12 January 2026.

111 In the Middle Ages the word 'livery' referred to the clothing, food and drink granted to the servants of great households. Later, it came to mean the emblem, badge or uniform of a corporate body.

112 Dates given in brackets refer to the company's first royal charter; many hold records indicating their existence from the twelfth and thirteenth centuries.

113 This is generally accepted, although the Woolmen have been known to ask, 'And who do you think you got your wool from?'.

114 The church, dating from the eleventh or twelfth century, stood in Laurence Pountney Lane, between Cannon Street and Upper Thames Street. It was destroyed in the Great Fire of 1666. St James Garlickhythe is now the Company's chosen church.

115 Frances Consitt, *The Weavers' Company of London* (Oxford, 1936), pp. 2–3.

116 The burellers, who sold English cloth, were most probably absorbed into the Drapers (who sold imported cloth) in the mid-fourteenth century (see Consitt, p. 32).

117 I am grateful to John Nugée, a past Upper Bailiff of the Worshipful Company of Weavers, for passing on this interpretation of events. 'The mayor,' he notes, 'was something of an anomaly; the position of mayor is nowhere mentioned in the original governance of London and he seems just to have emerged, and then later morphed into the *Lord* Mayor. The governance of the City was at the time in the hands of two sheriffs, then and still to this day elected by the livery (the elections are *not* choreographed or stage managed, and are not infrequently genuinely contested elections...). The position of the sheriffs, and Londoners' right to vote for them, is a privilege granted to London in Saxon times and confirmed by King William I in his famous letter to the inhabitants of London in 1067 – the oldest extant letter written by an English king to his subjects, and also one of the most astonishing.'.

118 Quoted in Consitt, *The Weavers' Company of London*, p. 36.

119 The details of this 160-year struggle can be found in Consitt, pp. 36–60. In the interests of balance, however, the author quotes a more positive account of the acceptance of foreigners into England: 'The almost immediate rise of the immigrants to prosperity was traditional in England. According to Fuller, they achieved wealth in a few years. "Happy the Yeoman's house into which one of these Dutch men did enter, bringing industry and wealth along with them. Such who came in strangers within their doors, soon after went out bridegrooms and returned sons in law, having married the daughters of the landlords who first entertained them. Yea, these Yeomen in whose houses they harboured soon proceeded gentlemen, gaining great estates to themselves, arms and worship to their estates." This atmosphere of friendliness was singularly lacking in London. The picture may be truer of provincial England. The foreigners had not the same opportunity to acquire wealth in the capital until their position was regularised' (Consitt, p. 39).

120 The price was £23 6s 8d, to be paid in three instalments over eighteen months (Consitt, pp. 162–3).

121 Consitt, pp. 157–61.

122 Consitt, pp. 164–5. The 'Masters' whose Parlour was used as an office were master weavers rather than officials of the Company. The Weavers' Hall survived until the Great Fire of 1666. It was rebuilt in 1667–9. In 1856–7 the old hall was demolished and the site at 22 Basinghall Street was redeveloped as offices. The site was damaged by German bombs on the night of 10 May 1941, and sold in 1961 (Alfred Plummer, *The London Weavers' Company 1600–1970* (London, 1972), pp. 192–4, 385–8, 407–9, 418–19).

123 Their time as soldiers was deducted from their seven-year term of apprenticeship.

124 William Watson died on 25 February 1673 and was 'buried from the Hall' with traditional honours (Plummer, pp. 255–7).

125 Plummer, p. 364.

126 Plummer, p. 354, and Chapter 16, 'An Early-Victorian Lord Mayor'.

127 Jonathan Ouvry, former Clerk and Upper Bailiff, email to the author, 16 August 2023.

128 The price was £9,000, and the sale completed by 8 May 1947. The authors are grateful to Sophie George and Penny Hunting for bringing this forgotten transaction to their attention.

129 Jonathan Ouvry, email to the author, 16 August 2023.

130 Jonathan Ouvry, interview with the author, 2 August 2023.

131 Worshipful Company of Weavers, *Upper Bailiff's Report 2025–2026*.

132 *Ibid.*

133 Ratification by Sir Nicholas Bacon, Sir Christopher Wraye and Sir James Dyer of the ordinances for regulating the Weaver's Guild, 25 June 1577 (Weavers' Company Muniments, A. 10), Item 12, quoted by Consitt, p. 292.

134 Plummer, p. 62.

The Textile Livery Group and Other Textile Guilds

The Textile Livery Group

Broderers

Clothworkers

Drapers

Dyers

Feltmakers

Framework Knitters

Gold and Silver Wyre Drawers

Haberdashers

Mercers

Merchant Taylors

UKFT

Weavers

Woolmen

Other Textile Guilds

The Aberdeen Weaver Incorporation

The Incorporation of Weavers, Fullers and Shearmen (Exeter)

The Incorporation of Weavers of Edinburgh

The Merchant Taylors Company of York

Shrewsbury Drapers Company

The Weaver Incorporation of Dundee (The Weaver Craft)

The Incorporation of Weavers of Glasgow

The Worshipful Company of Clothiers of Worcester

The Selkirk Incorporation of Weavers

Glossary

'A' level: a single subject studied at advanced level in the last two years of secondary school.

ARM 60: a small hand-operated loom made in Switzerland, widely used in the teaching of weaving and textile design.

BA: Bachelor of Arts; an undergraduate university degree in an arts subject.

bast fibres: fibres derived from the stems of plants such as flax, hemp, nettle and jute.

beam: a roller on which the warp threads are held. The warp beam unrolls as the weaving proceeds, while the cloth beam collects the woven fabric.

broadcloth: a dense, high-quality plain-woven cloth, weather-resistant and hard-wearing. It was woven wide, then milled with heavy hammers and hot soapy water to bind the fibres closer together.

BSc: Bachelor of Science; an undergraduate university degree in a scientific subject.

BTEC: short for Business and Technology Education; a vocational qualification at secondary school level or above, equivalent to an 'A' level or (in its highest form) the first year of a bachelor's degree in a practical subject.

BTech: short for Bachelor of Technology; an undergraduate degree in engineering.

dobby loom: a semi-automated loom that allows more complex weaving patterns than a treadle loom by picking up different groups of warp threads.

hopsack weave: a weave with two or more warp and weft threads interlaced in a loose, basket-like pattern.

Jacquard: a mechanism attached to a loom, which selects and lifts individual warp threads to create complex woven patterns and images. The mechanism, invented by the French weaver Joseph Marie Jacquard (1752–1834), is programmed with punched cards.

kersey: a coarse, cheap woollen cloth widely produced in medieval England.

livery company: one of more than 100 charitable organisations in the City of London founded on associations of trades and professions. Many were formed in the Middle Ages as guilds.

MA: Master of Arts; a postgraduate university degree.

rapier: a form of **shuttle** used on modern looms that carries the warp thread rapidly from one side of the cloth to the centre, where it is collected by another rapier coming from the far side.

sett: the number of warp threads per inch of fabric; also, the repeating pattern of lines and colours that make up a tartan.

shuttle: a wooden holder for the **weft** thread, pointed at both ends, passed from side to side of the loom to weave the fabric.

'T' level: a two-year technical qualification for 16–19-year-olds, combining classroom work with a placement in industry.

treadle loom: a loom operated by a seated weaver, who uses his or her feet to press treadles that lift alternate sections of the warp, allowing the shuttle to pass through.

twill: a dense, ribbed fabric with diagonal ridges made by passing the **weft** thread over one or more **warp** threads and then under two or more, with an offset between rows.

warp: the long parallel threads that form the longitudinal basis of a woven fabric. These are tied on to a **beam** at the opposite end of the loom from the weaver. The **weft** thread is passed from side to side using a **shuttle** or **rapier**.

warp float: a weaving pattern with warp threads lifted above the surface of the fabric to create design and texture.

warp-weighted loom: an early form of loom in which the warp threads hung vertically and were tensioned with weights.

weft: the thread that is passed across and between the **warp** threads to create the fabric.

worsted: a fine yarn spun from combed wool, which is woven to create smooth, lightweight fabrics.

Acknowledgements

Our heartfelt thanks go to all who gave interviews for this book, showing us their places of work in mills, studios and university departments, sharing their insights and experiences and the fabrics and designs they create.

We are particularly grateful to the staff of the Worshipful Company of Weavers – James Gaselee (Clerk), Anne Howe (Charities Officer) and Sophie George (Assistant to the Clerk) – and to the members of the Company who provided leads and ideas, and then read drafts of the text: Harriet Wallace-Jones, Julius Walters, Rebecca Ridley, Julian Radcliffe, Jonathan Ouvry, John Nugée, Richard Humphries, Gary Eastwood, James Dracup, George Courtauld and David Collinge. Discovering this remarkable industry with their guidance and support has been a fascinating and enlightening experience.

Image credits

A.W. Hainsworth 24; Alamy 41, 73, 155, 158, 192, 222 ; Alamy/Andrew Ray 69t; Alamy/Emily Marie Wilson 69b; Alamy/Horst Friedrichs 68b; Alamy/Nick Scott 40; Alex Begg 34l, 36; Arnolfini/Lisa Whiting 25, 140–1; Arville 86, 88, 90–1; Bridgeman/The National Gallery 191; Brighton and Hove Museums/Jim Holden 48–9; Philippa Brock 117, 119b, 119t; Bute Fabrics 66; Camira web page 95t, 98; Canterbury Cathedral/Jon Barlow 146; Catherine Chambers 131; Peter Cook 206; Crafts Study Centre 157; Crafts Study Centre collections, University for the Creative Arts, CWP/10/7/7 103; Emma Crichton-Miller 9, 14t, 110, 111, 169, 170l, 172, 173; David Cripps 106 (both); Dovecot Studios 208t; Rosemary and Penelope Ellis 210b; Lily Everard 159; @Fitzwilliam Museum, University of Cambridge 48l; Gainsborough's House/Jackie Mellor Photography 47; Sophie George 139; Getty Images/Bert Morgan 30; Gieves & Hawkes 46r; Guy Hills 148b, 148t, 150b, 150t, 151; Hainsworth 8; Circe Hamilton 116; Handweavers 215, 216; Claire Hardaker 217, 218, 219; Daniel Hearn 161tl; Heathcoat Fabrics 82, 85b; Minnie Hooper 194; Courtesy of Margaret Howell/Photography Matt Ford Studio 104–5; iStock.com/Sofia Zhuravets 84; W.T. Johnson 62; Johnstons of Elgin/James Merrell 16; @2025 The Josef and Anni Albers Foundation/DACS, London 100t; Jessica Jane Photography 171; M. Jessop 174, 175, 189; John Spencer Textiles 56–7, 58 (both), 59; Johnstons of Elgin 28, 29; Keith Hunter Photography 208b; François Laugénie/@Adagp, Paris 100b; Leeds Industrial Museum 53; Lochcarron 70, 71 (both), 72; The London Picture Archive 236; Lovat Mill 75 (both), 76; Jackson Tucker Lynch 68t; Ptolemy Mann 113, 114; Alex Martin 10l, 11, 14b, 18l, 18r, 19, 27, 34, 37, 38, 54, 60, 61, 63, 65, 67, 85m, 85t, 92, 93, 95b, 99, 132, 134, 145, 152, 161b, 170r, 177b, 177t, 178, 179, 181, 183, 185, 186, 187, 193, 221, 231, 234; Stanley Mills 77t; Mitchell 136; Abraham Moon 22–3; Montreal Centre for Contemporary Textiles 120; Moreland Primary School 195; Jane Mote 108; NASA/JPL-Caltech 78–9, 79r; New Designers/Mark Cocksedge 144; Nottingham Trent University 163, 164 (both), 165, 166, 167; One Wilkie Group 21; Rita Párniczky 128, 129; Onur Pinar 203; Eleanor Pritchard 204; Helen Rayner 205b; Ismini Samanidou 122, 123, 124, 125, 126; Science Museum Pictorial/Science Museum Group 80t; Margo Selby 147; Wallace Sewell 133b, 133t, 135, 137, 138; Shutterstock 196, 198; Society of Antiquaries 102; Niall Trowsdale Stannard 161tr; Yuki Sugiura 182; The Textile Centre of Excellence 199l, 200–1; The Textile Centre of Excellence/Kirsty Bowen 199r; Courtesy of Tiverton Museum of Mid Devon Life 80b; Shannon Tofts 207; Yeshen Venema 205t; @Veronika Speigl Photography 109; Waddesdon/National Trust, Bequest of James de Rothschild 232r; Stephen Walters 45, 46l; Reproduced by permission of the Warner Textile Archive, Braintree District Museum Trust 42, 43, 50r; WEFFAN 212, 213, 214; Wellcome Collection 10r, 12, 13; West Dean College 210t, 211; Wooltex 202; The Worshipful Company of Weavers 226, 230, 232l, 235l, 235r, 237, 239b, 239t, 240b, 240m, 240t, 241b, 241t; The Worshipful Company of Weavers/Victoria Jones 77b; The Worshipful Company of Weavers/Alex Martin 228; Humphries Weaving 17t, 50l; Edina van der Wyck 17b

Index

Page numbers in *italic* refer to illustrations and captions.